# THE MANUAL

of

# KARATE

E. J. HARRISON
(*Judo 4th Dan*)

LONDON
W. FOULSHAM & CO. LTD.
NEW YORK . TORONTO . CAPE TOWN . SYDNEY

*W. FOULSHAM & Co. Ltd*

*Yeovil Road, Slough, Berks, England*

New Revised Illustrated Edition
1974


ISBN 0 572 00063 4

© *E. J. Harrison 1959*

Printed in Great Britain at
The Pitman Press, Bath

# CONTENTS

1

**The Punch.**

2

3

4

**The Roundhouse Kick.**

2

1

3

5

**Knifehand Block.**

1

2

3

6

**Front Snap Kick.**

2

1

3

**Low Block.**

2

1

3

# AUTHOR'S PREFACE

Since confession is reputed to be good for that unverified abstraction, the soul, I may as well admit at the outset that I do not claim the distinction of originality for this little volume on the legendary Japanese art of karate. It may rather be described as an amalgam of two Japanese works on the subject, primarily the "Karate-Do Nyumon" or "Introduction to the Karate Way compiled by the Society for Study of Japanese Karate", and to a lesser degree "Karate no Narai-Kata" or "Methods of Study of Karate" by Reikichi Oya, an acknowledged authority on the art.

Although responsible for the translation of the Japanese original I have enjoyed the valuable collaboration of Mr. Taiyo Ono, himself a 3rd Dan in judo of the Kodokan, and at present on the staff of the Japanese language section of the BBC, in the final revision of the English text, the clarification of many obscure and doubtful passages, and the confirmation that the English terminology does justice to its parent Japanese. And I am glad here to acknowledge my indebtedness to him under this head.

On the merits of karate I shall not at this stage descant. The better plan will be to let this book speak for itself. Nevertheless it would be unrealistic to ignore the fact that comparisons between judo and karate alike as sports and fighting arts are bound to be instituted and are indeed already making themselves heard. In my opinion in determining this issue much depends upon what the neophyte himself hopes to derive from the study and practice of either. Perhaps the operation of "vested interests" will interpose an insuperable obstacle to the eventual integration of both these arts which I have reason to believe the followers of karate, both Japanese and non-Japanese, regard as a consummation "devoutly to be wished". Only time will show. Yet in at least one branch of judo, atemiwaza, karate has demonstrated how immeasurably more deadly and efficacious methods of attacking vital spots (kyusho) can be made if the disciple adopts the drastic karate system of tempering and toughening the

9

natural members employed for that purpose, e.g. the fingers, hands, fists, elbows, knees, heels, toes and soles. Elsewhere in these pages I have indicated the main "particulars" in the inductive process which undoubtedly differentiate karate from judo. Speaking for myself alone I would say that nothing I have latterly learnt about karate has in the slightest degree diminished my regard for the latter as a high-class sport based upon an ethical concept. And, of course, in both these arts the element of esotericism bulks largely. But even my limited knowledge of karate culled from printed and oral testimony suffices to convince me that if the candidate wants to be equipped a hundred per cent for fighting without lethal weapons, then he cannot afford to exclude practical knowledge of karate from his defensive and offensive repertoire. And in this context I feel convinced that our police and military would be well advised to avail themselves of opportunities for learning karate so as to be better able to cope with a sudden emergency. Meanwhile we know that in the USA the importance and value of karate as a fighting art are recognized in such high quarters as the SAC (Strategic Air Command) which periodically sends picked teams of its best men to Japan for refresher courses in the art to supplement their skill in judo and thus ensure their ability to tackle, even when otherwise unarmed, suspicious and obstreperous characters inclined to be bellicose and to resist arrest.

It should however be noted that even Reikichi Oya warns us against much of the grandiloquent writing devoted to the art by some of its over-enthusiastic pioneers. All in all a fair and well-balanced judgement would seem to be that after a salutary process of deflation of much hyperbole we are entitled to accept the art for what it clearly is, a unique system of fighting with the bare hands and feet in both self-defence and counter-attack.

E.J.H.

# CHAPTER I

## KARATE ORIGINS—FACT AND FICTION—CONFIRMED AND ALLEGED FEATS OF FAMOUS KARATE MASTERS—ADVANTAGES OF KARATE FOR OLD AND YOUNG

THE word karate itself literally means "empty hand" (kara= empty, te=hand). It is pronounced "kah-rah-teh". Although like jujutsu the early origins of the art are traced to China, it owes its development to the inhabitants of the Luchu Islands which are situated approximately 200 miles to the south-west of Japan. The name Luchu is pronounced Ryukyu by the Japanese. At the beginning of the seventeenth century the islands were conquered by the Japanese under the Daimyo of Satsuma. The Luchuans continued to pay tribute to both China and Japan till 1879 when the king was brought captive to Tokyo and the government was reorganized as a Japanese prefecture under the style of Okinawa Ken, as it has since been called. Like their Chinese predecessors the Japanese conquerors would not allow the natives to carry weapons of any kind. But for their self-protection against their alien oppressors the natives cleverly circumvented this ukase by devising and elaborating the system of bare-hand fighting now known as karate. Then in our own day, as mentioned in the new edition of my book, "The Fighting Spirit of Japan", it was the famous Okinawa karate master Funakoshi who introduced it into Japan proper as karate-do, or the "way" of karate. In this altered name we can detect an analogy with judo in which the word "do", meaning "way" was substituted by the late Dr. Jigoro Kano, the founder of judo, to emphasize the ethical basis of his new eclectic system of self-defence. Thus the present-day protagonists of karate are equally insistent on the purpose of their art as a means not of aggression but of self-defence over and above its alleged value as a system of physical culture par excellence. And although not denying the ability of trained karateka to smash boards, pulverize tiles and bricks and pierce bamboo fences with their hardened bare hands and finger-tips, they deprecate unilateral

11

absorption in the purely physical attributes of karate to the exclusion of its alleged spiritual rationale. It is even contended that certain movements of the karate katas or forms are specially designed to purify the performer's spirit and are therefore congruent with the maxim *"Karate ni sente nashi"* which can be freely interpreted to mean that there is no first attack in karate. In other words the karateka is careful to observe Polonius's sage counsel to his son Laertes, "Beware of entrance to a quarrel but being in, bear't that the opposed may beware of thee." Only in the last resort and when realizing that he would otherwise fail to champion the cause of justice and humanity (*seigi jindo*, in Japanese) should the karateka decide to stage the first attack.

Further evidence of the desire of karate's responsible leadership to discourage the prominence currently given to the physical manifestations of the art can be discerned in Reikichi Oya's timely reminder that there is a considerable difference between a static wooden board, a heap of tiles or bricks, and a living, moving, perhaps armed, opponent bent upon putting you to your earthly account at close quarters. In this context one is tempted to paraphrase the immortal Pierre, "the bravest man in France," when taunting the equally immortal Thomas Winterbottom Hance of Old England, that motionless boards and bricks "give no retaliating thwack" and "don't ever hit you back." This nice distinction is one which all aspiring karateka will do well to bear in mind when they are beyond the boundaries of their dojos.

Judo is called "the way of gentleness," whereas our author complains that karate is often dubbed "the power way." But is the latter definition warranted? Certainly in karate the full power of the body is invoked when a blow is dealt but this fact represents only one facet of the truth. It would be incomplete if it left out of account the many occasions when small but well-trained karateka have defeated opponents vastly their superior in physical strength and when karate veterans have easily disposed of powerful but inexperienced youngsters.

Although doubtless many of the amazing stories recounted about past karate masters may be dismissed as apocryphal, the authenticity of modern versions can be vouched for. Indeed it so happens that I have in my possession visual proof of the ability of Japanese karateka to split and pulverize boards, tiles and bricks with their bare hands. This is contained in a striking article contributed by a writer named Jay Gluck to the Sydney weekly "People" of January 22, 1958. It is in effect an account of his visit to a well-known karate dojo in Tokyo. Among the photographs reproduced is one showing an expert in the act of breaking a clump of bricks with a sharp bare-handed blow, and another expert breaking nine roofing tiles with his right elbow. We are assured that a professional can crack seventeen and can break half a dozen with a blow of his head! Another photograph shows an expert in the act of smashing three three-quarter-inch thick squares of pliable practice board with his closed hand. The karateka's feet are equally formidable weapons. Thus one photograph shows a karateka practising the backward kick against a post. Hundreds of repetitions of this style of kicking turn a man's heel into a deadly instrument. These photographs reveal the abnormal development of the karateka's feet. In one of them we are shown a karateka in the act of defending himself against a dagger attack. It is assumed that the expert would succeed in thrusting aside the hoodlum's dagger arm and that his ensuing "foot punch" could easily break the assailant's thigh in two. The manner in which the karateka's limbs are tempered and toughened to the degree required for the accomplishment of such feats is described elsewhere in these pages.

Turning to the annals of the old time karate masters I will give precedence to an uncanny esoteric karate method of condemning the victim to deferred deaths called "san-nen-goroshi" and "ju-nen-goroshi", meaning respectively "three-year-kill" and "ten-year-kill".

It is asserted that the master of this "hiho" or secret method could deal the victim a blow with his fist from which the victim would not at the time experience any physical discomfort but that three or ten years later the affected part of his body would become daily more and more painful until in the end he would die! Another alleged "hiho" is called the "niku-sen-kiri", literally "flesh cut into a thousand pieces". This is the metaphorical name of a method whereby the karate expert could plunge his tempered finger-tips into the body of his victim and pluck out not perhaps so many as a thousand pieces of flesh but enough of them to ensure his victim's almost instantaneous dissolution!

13

I shall end this introduction in a lighter vein with a summary of the advantages officially claimed for karate: (1) Old people and children, men and women, can practise it. (2) It can be practised almost anywhere without special equipment. (3) It can be practised at almost any time and any hour but naturally subject to human needs. (4) Given ordinary care no danger is involved. (5) It can be practised singly or in company with others. Young and old men, both sexes without distinction, even those physically weak, without overtaxing themselves may safely practise it.

The kata or forms constitute the nucleus of karate practice. But it is contended that the karate kata differ from those of judo or sumo in that the performer can at his discretion suitably regulate the degree of strength needed for their execution. Thus the physically powerful performer can give an exhibition replete with force while the weak performer can adapt his display to his individual capacity and execute the kata lightly. Or again the strong man is at liberty to infuse an optional amount of strength into his demonstration in accordance with the daily condition of his body. In this manner the limitations of sex are taken into consideration and even when he or she suffers from certain physical disabilities he or she can easily practise karate. Then again, seeing that there are as many as thirty different kinds of kata in present-day karate, the performer can at any time choose those to his liking and freely execute a given number.

In this context, we are assured, innumerable examples could be adduced of persons originally weak who, having taken up the practice of karate as a means of self-preservation, have eventually changed almost out of recognition into strong and well-built individuals.

As already briefly mentioned, no special premises are required for the practice of karate. If a mat-covered floor is not available an ordinary boarded floor will do equally well. Or an open space of ground, say in a garden or courtyard, will suffice for the execution of the karate kata. On the other hand, considering the speedy tempo with which karate seems to be gathering momentum in the West, it is a fair guess that before long recourse to such makeshift expedients will not be necessary and that regular dojos or exercise halls, as in Japan, will become available.

14

# CHAPTER II

STRUCTURE OF KARATE—METHODS OF CLENCHING THE FIST
—EMPI OR HIJIATE—HAND TECHNIQUES OR TEWAZA

IN the parlance of all karate schools the fist is called the "soul" of that art. Special attention must therefore be devoted to the "tempering" or hardening of the fist in order to enhance the efficacy of the blows dealt with it, held in various ways. Below are summarized and illustrated the more important of these methods. In accordance with the now accepted practice in most books on judo I give the relevant terminology in both its original Japanese and English.

SEIKEN *(normal fist):* There are two methods. Thus in Fig. 1a the hand is shown with the thumb held outside. The four

Fig. I A                    Fig. I B

finger-tips as far as their roots are joined together in such a way that the first and second joints form a plane.

Fig. 1b shows the hand held with the thumb slightly raised and all four finger-tips pressed into the palm. Fig. 1c shows

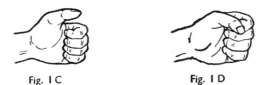

Fig. I C                    Fig. I D

the thumb held lower with the four fingers bent, and Fig. 1d shows the thumb bent over the first finger and all four fingers pressed into the palm. Figs. 2 and 3 demonstrate two variants of the clenched fist, viz., the fist with the thumb bent over the forefinger and the second with the forefinger extended and pressed into the palm somewhat lower down than the other three fingers. And in this connection the Japanese author impresses on the student that the fist should always be held tightly clenched; otherwise, if the fingers are too

Fig. 2

Fig. 3 A

Fig. 3 B

loose when he strikes his opponent, he may incur the risk of injury. The part used for attack with the seiken or normal fist comprises the roots of the forefinger and middle finger (Fig. 3a). So much for the moment for the normal fist.

HIRAKEN *(flat or level fist):* In this method the four fingers are arranged shallowly clasped. The thumb tip presses against the side of the forefinger. The part used for attack comprises the second joints of the forefinger and middle finger (Fig. 4). As a rule the target of attack is the opponent's face.

URAKEN *(back fist):* Fig. 5 shows the fist thus held. In this

Fig. 4

Fig. 5

Fig. 6

position the root of the middle finger is generally used to attack the opponent's face.

KENTSUI *(hammer fist):* In this position the lower part of the edge of the palm is used for attack and symbolizes the so-called hammer fist (Fig. 6). While beating off the opponent's wrist the head of the fist and the hard part of the joints can be used for attack.

HITOSASHIYUBI-IPPONKEN *(forefinger fist):* The fist is held in the hiraken fashion with the knuckle of the forefinger thrust forward. It is used to attack the opponent's solar-plexus (suigetsu) and the vital spot (kyusho) just under the nose called jinchu in Japanese. The English anatomical equivalent is the philtrum (Fig. 7).

16

NAKAYUBI-IPPONKEN *(middle finger fist)*: With the fist held in the normal fist (seiken) style the middle finger knuckle is projected. This method is used to attack the opponent's solar-plexus and jinchu (Fig. 8).

Fig. 7                    Fig. 8

TEGATANA, sometimes called SHUTO *(handsword)*: and NUKITE *(piercing hand)*: (1) *Four-finger Piercing Hand:* In this method the thumb is bent while the other four fingers are adjusted evenly and extended as shown in Fig. 9. The four finger-tips are used to thrust into the opponent's solar-plexus, his sides, etc. In the same connection we get the tate-nukite or lengthwise piercing hand in which the back of the hand is turned sideways, the fingers aligned lengthwise and used

Fig. 9                    Fig. 10

in this shape, and the hira-nukite or level piercing hand with the back of the hand turned upwards and the fingers held sideways. (2) *Two-finger Piercing Hand:* In this method the ring finger, the little finger and the thumb are bent and the forefinger and the middle finger extended (Fig. 10). This method is generally used to attack the opponent's eyes. (3) *One-finger Piercing Hand:* In this method only the

Fig. 11                    Fig. 12

forefinger is stretched out and also used to thrust at the opponent's eyes (Fig. 11). (4) TEGATANA *(handsword)*: In this method the thumb is bent and the four fingers are extended. About two-thirds of the base of the palm are used in much the

17

same way as the hammer fist (Fig. 12). In this manner the handsword can be used to attack the opponent's carotid arteries, his arms, temples, middle of forehead, the jinchu, etc. But in that case you must be careful not to let the root of the little finger be applied to the objective. (5) *Base of palm:* The palm is opened, the first joint of the thumb bent and attached to the surface of the palm. In this position the base of the palm is used to attack the opponent's face, his shoulders, chest, &c. with an upraised thrusting movement (Fig. 13). (6) In this style the thumb is bent deeply into the center of the palm and the spot marked black in Fig. 14 used

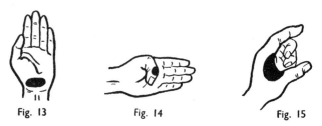

Fig. 13         Fig. 14         Fig. 15

to deal an upward thrusting blow from under the opponent's jaw. Or the lateral surface of the same spot on the thumb can also be used for the same purpose. (7) HIRA-HASAMI (*Literally "Flat Scissors"*) : In this method the middle finger, ring finger and little finger are slightly bent so that the forefinger and thumb form as it were a pair of scissors. When in action the lateral surface of the thumb and forefinger is used to strike your opponent's neck muscles (Fig. 15). (8) YUBI-HASAMI (*finger scissors):* The middle finger, ring finger and little finger are deeply bent, leaving the thumb and forefinger to assume the so-called scissor shape. In action the middle finger and thumb are thrust against your opponent's throat and it is also possible to use the "scissors" of the thumb and forefinger to choke your opponent (Fig. 16). (9) YUMI-KOBUSHI (*bow fist):* The thumb and forefingers are extended with the tips held downwards, the wrist strongly bent upwards as shown in Fig. 17 to form the so-called "bow". The blackened point on the upturned wrist is chiefly used to parry blows. (10) KOTE (*forearm):* This is used to ward off an opponent's attack. For this purpose the forearm is used in three ways, each of which has its own designation. First is the outer forearm or omote-

18

kote, also called the inner forearm or thumb edge; second, the reverse or rear forearm, ura-kote, also called the outside forearm, i.e. the little finger edge, and third, the level forearm,

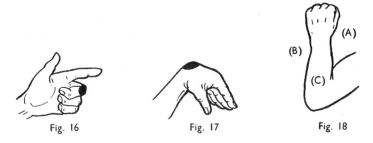

Fig. 16      Fig. 17      Fig. 18

hira-kote, or center of the outer and inner forearm, otherwise the back of the outer and reverse forearms (Fig. 18). These three divisions are marked *a*, *b* and *c* in the illustration.

EMPI *(literally "outstretched arm")* HIJIATE, *or Elbow Attacks:*

In karate the elbow is used to assail your opponent's solar-plexus, chest and abdomen. And we are assured that given adequate training even a weak woman or a child could in an emergency make effective use of that natural weapon. (1) TATE-EMPI *(vertical empi):* In this posture you stand with your fists touching your hip and your elbow held upwards. If both elbows are held upwards then the technical term is "ryo-tate-empi" or "both-vertical-empi". (2) SAGETA EMPI *(lowered empi):* In this posture your elbows are held downwards in readiness for attack or hijiate. (3) ZEN EMPI *(frontal empi):* The fist is held close to the back of the head as if in the act of carrying something, and for attack the elbow is brought forward. (4) KO-EMPI *(rear empi):* This is one of the most frequently used methods of an elbow attack or hijiate. The fist is brought up about as far as the ear but then apparently lowered since the author adds that it touches the hip in such a way that if you happen to be hugged from behind by your opponent you can drive your elbow (presumably the right) with maximum force into his solar-plexus. (5) ZENGO EMPI *(front and rear empi):* When attacked by two opponents from the front and rear respectively you bring both

19

your left and right elbows into play apparently against the solar-plexus. (6) YOKO-EMPI *(lateral empi):* In this method the right or left fist and elbow are held horizontally, then brought in front of the chest in order to deliver a lateral elbow attack. If both elbows are used the method is called "ryo-yoko-empi". (7) HINERI-YOKO-EMPI *(twisting-lateral-empi):* In this method both fists are held with the thumb edges at the side of both breasts and the elbow opened. The shoulders should not be spread but kept well lowered. In this posture the upper part of your body can be twisted to the right or left and your right or left elbow used simultaneously against the solar-plexus of an enemy attacking from the side or rear. It may be possible to have recourse to this method if attacked by very strong opponents.

## HAND TECHNIQUES OR TEWAZA

Hand techniques comprise tsukite or thrusting hand, tegatana or handsword, already mentioned in the preceding section, nukite or piercing hand, ukete or defending hand, haraite or sweeping hand, &c. These and other methods are briefly described below.

1. TSUKITE: *(thrusting hand):* This together with ukete is the most frequently utilized form of Tewaza. The hand should be instantly withdrawn after delivery of the thrust to avert the risk of being countered.

2. UKETE: *(defence hand):* This method is used as a defence against an enemy's hand or leg attack. It is classified into several branches such as the jodan-uke, meaning literally the upper-step defence but for practical purposes the upper body; the chudan-uke, middle-step or middle body defence; and the gedan-uke, lower-step or lower body defence. Every uke is further divided into uchi-uke or inner uke and soto-uke or outer uke, also termed omote-uke and ura-uke. To this category also pertain numerous variants (henka). For example, there are the ude-uke or arm-uke in which the fist is half clenched, the tegatana-uke or handsword uke in which the four fingers are stretched and the thumb bent for defence, the yoko-uke or lateral uke, &c.

3. HARAITE *(sweeping hand):* This is one kind of ukete in which you defend yourself by beating off an opponent's

20

hand or leg attack. There are also the sub-divisions called uchi-barai (literally "sweeping-off"), the tegatana-barai (hand-sword sweep), &c.

4. YUMI-UKE *(bow uke)*: In this method, by means of the bow fist (yumi-kobushi) already described, you spring up your assailant's thrusting hand from underneath and so ward off his attack. This is also a type of ukete.

5. KAKETE *(literally "hook-hand")*: This is also a type of ukete whereby you intercept an opponent's hand thrust.

6. HIKITE *(pull hand)*: This is a variant of the hook hand. The instant you parry your opponent's thrusting hand (tsukite) you grasp his hand and pull it towards you. The pull hand enables you to disturb your opponent's posture, thus blocking his offensive and rendering your counter-attack more efficacious.

7. HINERITE *(twisting hand)*: This is a variant of the hikite. However, you do not simply pull your opponent towards you but while twisting him in the opposite direction you also attack him.

8. DAKITE *(hugging hand)*: A kind of ukete. You grasp your opponent's thrusting hand, pull it towards you and under your arm but afterwards attack in your turn.

9. SUKUITE *(scooping hand)*: A kind of ukete whereby you scoop up your opponent's hand or leg and perhaps throw him. His attacking hand and leg are blocked and his posture is disturbed.

10. KAKIWAKE *(thrust aside)*: Say for example that your opponent attacks with a both hands (morote) thrust, then with your left and right wrist you dash it aside.

11. UCHITE *(striking hand)*: This method is used for both attack and defence. For example, in attack you can use the hammer fist (kentsui), handsword (tegatana) &c., to hit your opponent's vital spots. Or in defence you can again use the hammer fist (kentsui), the wrist or the handsword to strike his attacking hand or foot and so shatter his offensive power.

The foregoing methods may help to exemplify some of the more effective hand techniques (tewaza) used to attack an opponent or to thwart his attack, to block his efforts to disturb your balance and to facilitate your plan to nullify his offensive and so subject him completely to your control.

## CHAPTER III

### WAYS OF PLANTING THE FEET OR ASHI-NO-TACHI-KATA

IN the kata or forms of karate, more particularly the preparatory postures, three basic kinds are specified, i.e. musubitachi
or linked posture, heisokutachi or blocked foot posture, and
hachijitachi or figure-eight posture. These are in turn sub-
divided into the soto-hachijitachi or the outer figure-eight
posture and the uchi-hachijitachi or the inner figure-eight
posture. Furthermore in demonstrations of the karate katas
or forms we have the zenkutsutachi or inclined posture, the
kokutsutachi or retroflex posture, the fudotachi or immobile
posture, the neko-ashitachi or cat foot posture, the kibatachi
or equestrian posture, &c. Below I have attempted to describe
these several foot positions.

1. MUSUBITACHI *(linked feet):* The left and right heels are
joined with the tips of the toes turned outwards (Fig. 19a).

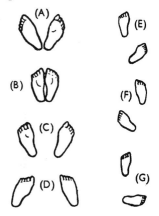

Fig. 19

This is a pose reminiscent of gymnastics but strength is not
infused into the shoulders and both arms are allowed to hang
naturally against the sides and the eyes gaze to the front.

2. HEISOKUTACHI *(blocked foot posture):* In this pose the
feet are drawn together up to the tips of the toes (Fig. 19b).

3. HACHIJITACHI (figure - eight posture): When standing in the soto-hachijitachi or the outer figure-eight posture, the tips of your toes are widely opened (Fig. 19c) and in the uchi-hachijitachi or inner figure of eight posture your heels are widely spread (Fig. 19d). The space between both heels depends upon the individual but generally it coincides with the space between the shoulders, say about seventeen inches.

4. *The "re"* ( ∫ ) *Letter Posture:* There are two positions, viz., left and right. The right "re" position is illustrated in Fig. 19e and the left "re" position in Fig. 19f.

5. TEI ( **T** ) *Letter Posture:* The position of the feet resembles the Japanese ideograph **T** ; hence its name (Fig. 19g).

Fig. 20                    Fig. 21

Figs. 20 and 21 are illustrations of a karateka standing with his feet planted in the Fig. 19b and 19c styles, respectively.

6. ZENKUTSUTACHI (inclined posture): In this position the space between your feet will differ according to your height but generally speaking it is about 2 feet 5 inches. The advanced right leg is bent so that from the knee to the heel it is almost perpendicular. The rear left leg is extended and the weight of the body is evenly distributed on both legs (Fig. 22).

7. KOKUTSUTACHI (retroflex posture): This is a posture

23

the reverse of the zenkutsutachi. Thus in this case your rear left leg is bent so that from the knee to the heel it is approximately perpendicular. Your forward right leg is outstretched. The weight of your body rests on your rear leg and the space between both feet is about 2 feet 5 inches (Fig. 23).

8. NEKO-ASHITACHI *(cat foot posture)*: Here your weight rests on your rear bent leg while your front leg is also bent but with the heel raised from the ground and the toes lightly applied to it. This posture is regarded as suitable for advance

Fig. 22                    Fig. 23                    Fig. 24

and retreat (shintai) or the execution of the kerikomi (kick-in), kerihanashi (kick release), &c. (Fig. 24).

9. SAGI-ASHITACHI *(heron leg posture)*: In this position one foot is lifted about as high as your other knee. If the lifted leg comes in front of the knee the posture is called mae-sagi-ashitachi or front heron leg posture; if behind, the ushiro-sagi-ashitachi or rear heron leg posture (Fig. 25).

10. KIBATACHI *(equestrian posture)*: In the somewhat cryptic karate terminology this posture is also called the naifu-anchi-tachi or anti-knife posture. The toes of both your feet are turned slightly inwards with the heels opened more than the toes. Strength is infused into the inner sides of the thighs. Both knees are adequately bent so that from the knees downwards the leg is almost perpendicular. Again strength is infused into the outer edge of the soles of both feet. Your upper body is held upright, both shoulders lowered, the chest extended, the hips dropped and power infused into

the lower abdomen familiar to all judo students under its Japanese name of saika tanden (Fig. 26).

11. SHIKOTACHI *(four thigh posture):* In this posture,

Fig. 25          Fig 26                    Fig. 27

differing from the kibatachi, your toes and knee-caps are turned outwards, i.e., as in the outer figure - eight posture (soto-hachijitachi); both your legs are widely opened, both

Fig. 28                        Fig. 29

knees bent, the upper body held upright and the hips dropped (Fig. 27).

12. SANSENTACHI *(three battle posture):* Emanating from the kibatachi and in that style you stand so that either the

left or right foot is brought forward the distance from the toes to the heel (Fig. 28).    The toes of both right and left foot point in the same direction.

13.    FUDOTACHI *(immobile posture):* In this posture your legs are a little more widely opened than in the zenkutsutachi. Both knees are adequately bent and both legs on an average equally share the weight of the body. (Fig. 29).

# CHAPTER IV

## LEG AND FOOT TECHNIQUES OR ASHIWAZA— PARTS OF FOOT USED IN KICKING

THE roots of the toes at the bottom of a raised foot when the toes are curved are likened to a pigeon's chest (Fig. 30). They should be the equivalent of the normal fist (seiken) and constitute the basis of keriwaza or kicking techniques. When the foot is being used to kick forward with the toes adequately curved, if strength is not infused into the ankle there is risk of injury so that care in this respect should always be taken.

2. *Bottom of foot:* Part of the heel on the under surface of the foot. It performs a very useful supplementary function when, for example, you tread powerfully down upon your opponent's instep, when delivering the keriage or upward kick, the kerihanashi or kick release, &c. (Fig. 31).

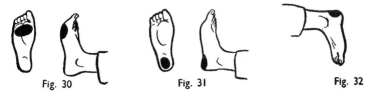

Fig. 30    Fig. 31    Fig. 32

3. USHIROKAKATO *(back heel):* This is used for the ushirogeri or rear kick (Fig. 32). When, for example, your waist is encircled from behind or your hand is twisted in the reverse direction the rear kick can be effectively used against your opponent's scrotum, shin, &c.

4. ASHIGATANA *(footsword):* As in the case of the bottom of the raised foot you curve the toes upward and use the little-toe edge of the foot for the fumikomi or step-in, the kerihanashi or kick release, the yokogeri or lateral kick, &c., to attack your opponent's knee joints, flank, &c. Care must be taken not to apply the root of the little toe. The ashigatana corresponds to the tegatana among the hand techniques (Fig. 33).

5. ASHIZOKO *(literally "foot bottom", to all intents and*

27

purposes the sole of the foot): With the so-called flat of the foot you sweep away the opponent's foot or ward off his thrusting fist. This method is not illustrated.

6. ASHIKUBI *(ankle):* Your toes are stretched in a straight line with your shin, in which position with the ankle you kick your opponent's scrotum (Fig. 34).

7. Toes and ankle are stretched in a straight line in which position you employ the maegeri or frontal kick to attack your opponent's solar-plexus, lower abdomen, &c. Not illustrated.

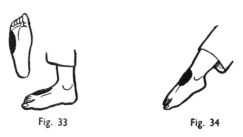

Fig. 33                    Fig. 34

8. HIZAGASHIRA *(knee-cap):* Can be effectively used to bash the scrotum of an approaching opponent.

Hand and foot techniques may be said to constitute the kernel of karate. Thus Reikichi Oya likens them to the two wheels of the Japanese jinrikisha. Both your hands and feet must be equally tempered, and unless this is done you may not hope to achieve perfection. And in this context, without in any way descending to invidious comparisons, we are entitled to claim that foot techniques are almost a monopoly of karate. Nevertheless it is essential that both branches should keep abreast of each other, running along parallel lines to ensure the ceaseless development of this remarkable art, and that to this end, as already emphasized, both the upper and lower limbs should be thoroughly toughened.

1. KERIHANASHI *(kick release):* Supporting your body on one leg with the other foot you kick your opponent's lower jaw, abdomen, shins or scrotum. Then with the maximum speed you must withdraw the attacking foot because otherwise he may succeed in scooping up your leg. No time therefore must be lost in reverting to your initial position so that your opponent has no chance to take advantage of you. The bottom of the foot is the part most used for the kick release.

2. KERIKOMI *(kick-in)*: In principle the kerikomi resembles the kerihanashi, but the kicking foot without reverting to its former position is used to step strongly against your opponent's knee-joint so as to dislocate it. When the foot is not used to kick but only to step in, this method is called simply fumikomi or step-in. This method is not illustrated.

3. KERIAGE *(upward kick)*: This method largely resembles in essentials the kerihanashi. With the sole of the foot you kick up your opponent's scrotum, &c., or stretching the ankle you can apply it for the same purpose. Not illustrated.

4. YOKOGERI *(lateral kick)*: Opposed to an adversary attacking you from the flank the ashigatana (footsword) can be used to deliver a kerihanashi. Again, sometimes without the kerihanashi the step-in (fumikomi) can be utilized. The manner of kicking is for you to stand on either the right or left foot, then draw up the sole to the region of either the left or right knee-cap (Fig. 35), then to the side deliver a power-

Fig. 35          Fig. 36

ful kick against the opponent's knee-joint or side of chest, &c. in the kerihanashi style (Fig. 36) and then instantly draw back your foot to its original position.

5. TOBIGERI *(jumping kick)*: In this method you leap up with both feet and kick your opponent's face, chest, &c. with either your left or right foot. Thus your object is to take him by surprise in order to hit the target. Unless the kicking action is swiftly and nimbly performed your leg may be

29

scooped up by your antagonist and when it comes down to the ground attacked in the opposite direction.

6. USHIROGERI *(rear kick):* If you are clasped from behind you may bend the knee and with the back heel kick up your opponent's shin, scrotum, &c.

7. KERIGAESHI *(return kick):* Simultaneously with your kerihanashi against your opponent's attacking hand or leg, with that foot you kick up at your opponent. Also when your kerihanashi is parried by your opponent, then without returning your leg to its original position you again execute a kerihanashi and then kick in.

8. MAWASHI-GERI *(turning kick):* When your opponent advances to attack from the left or right and as you use your left or right hand to tackle him, while you turn your body you lash out with the sole of your right or left foot against his scrotum, stomach, knee, &c. with the turning kick.

9. HIZATSUI *(knee hammer):* While grappling with an opponent you may be able to use your knee-cap to jab up his scrotum, &c.

10. FUMIKIRI *(step out):* Using the ashigatana (footsword) method described earlier, with the sensation of stepping out you kick in your opponent's leg.

11. FUMITSUKI *(tread on):* With the sole of your foot you stamp upon your opponent's instep and either thrust or push him down.

12. FUMIUCHI *(step blow):* When grappled from behind and using the base of either foot you impose the weight of your entire body to step upon your opponent's instep.

13. NAMIGAESHI *(wave change):* When your opponent is dealing a kick at your scrotum, &c. you use the sole of your foot to beat off the attacking foot.

14. TOBIGOSHI *(jumping over):* In the case of a surprise attack by an opponent armed with a club or stick with which to attack a leg, a trained karateka might be able to leap over his head and turning to the rear strike at the desired spot.

15. YORIASHI *(approaching leg):* Your opponent may be rather far off and while preserving the position of his hand and feet approach you with mincing steps so that in order to avoid his attack you recede also with mincing steps.

16. TOBIKOMIASHI *(jumping-in leg):* When your opponent is some distance away from you, the moment you observe a

gap you should suddenly jump in for the purpose of applying an effective technique.

17. NAGEASHI *(throw leg):* This term applies to a technique designed to throw your opponent.

18. MIKKATSUKI *(literally "Three-day Moon"):* When your opponent advances from the left or right to strike with his right or left fist, then while defending yourself with your left or right hand from the inner side you grasp his right or left wrist and as you pull him towards you, with your right or left foot you kick his chest. For some cryptic reason the action of kicking is likened to the drawing of a "three-day moon" (mikkatsuki).

19. SANKAKUTOBI *(triangular jump):* This technique is in the prolific karate repertoire designated a "divine technique" (kamiwaza) which admirably exemplifies the "mystery" of the art. It is assumed that you are simultaneously attacked by three adversaries. Keeping your body parallel with the surface of the ground you take a running leap and in the first place kick one of your assailants. The next one you resist with your fist and head and the third with a right or left foot kick. This explanation would benefit by a little more "corroborative detail" and something must be left to the reader's imagination in order to fill in the gaps.

CHAPTER V

AUXILIARY APPARATUS FOR TRAINING—THE MAKIWARA—
METHODS OF TEMPERING THE HANDS AND FEET—USE OF THE
KAKETEBIKI AND OTHER APPLIANCES—AUXILIARY EXERCISES

IN both the kątas or forms and kumite or contest of karate
it is essential that you should on no account neglect the
assiduous training of your natural weapons by means of the
special auxiliary apparatus recommended for that purpose.
If you do, then the real power and efficacy of the art will be
reduced by half. Below I have tried to describe as briefly and
simply as possible the principal items of this auxiliary
equipment.

1. THE MAKIWARA: For the training and hardening of
hands and feet — the parts of the body most often used for
attack in karate—this implement certainly ranks as the most
important. The two types most frequently installed are the
fixed and movable makiwara. The fixed type of makiwara
consists of a post about seven feet four inches long, of square
timber, preferably cypress because of its elasticity and resistance to wind and rain. Lacking cypress cedar is a good
substitute. The width of the post is about three or four inches.
The post is fixed in the earth to a depth of a little more than
two feet, and as a preservative against decay the buried
portion and about five or six inches above the ground should
be treated with coal tar. Special care must be taken to ensure
the stability of the post by strengthening the buried portion
with a casing of brick, &c. and the earth surrounding the post
on the surface can usefully be sprinkled with water and then
beaten down tightly with a stick or human feet. Fig. 38 gives a
good idea of what the makiwara looks like when in position.
Fig. 37 has been omitted as superfluous. Next comes the attach-
ment of the distinctive contrivance from which the makiwara
derives its name, viz., "sheaved straw". Fig. 39 should be
studied in this connection. The length of the straw rope bind-
ing is about one foot two inches, and its thickness about three
inches. The straw rope is firmly wound round a bundle of

straw and then beaten with a hammer or stick to flatten it, after which it is attached to the post as shown in Fig. 38. Two of these straw bundles are attached to the post, the upper one being intended for hardening the hands and the lower one for hardening the feet. The sketch also shows that the post gradually thickens from top to bottom. The idea is to preserve the

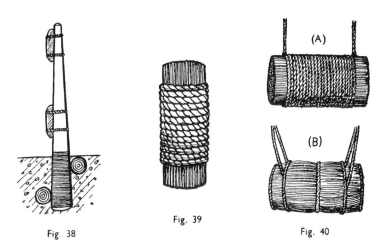

Fig. 38

Fig. 39

Fig. 40

resilience of the post and thus minimize the risk of injury to a bone or sinew when the karateka strikes the makiwara. The upper part of the makiwara serves to toughen the seiken (normal fist), hiraken (level fist), uraken (rear fist), kentsui (hammer fist), the forearm, tegatana (handsword), base of palm, yumiken (bow fist), &c. The lower part of the makiwara serves to toughen the ashigatana (footsword), &c.

For the special hardening of the hands and feet and developing the power of the hips and loins there are two other types of portable makiwara. Fig. 40a shows the type of makiwara designed to train and harden the hands and feet. It resembles the type used in Japanese archery (kyudo). The straw is cut to a length of about two feet and one foot in diameter. Three-ply straw rope should be used to bind it together and to both ends are attached straw ropes with which to hang the apparatus at about the height of a man's chest. The weight of the entire apparatus will be approximately 22 lbs. avoirdupois. Fig. 40b shows the contrivance used to strengthen the hips and loins. A strong linen sack is filled with sand or sawdust to a weight of approximately 40 lbs. avoirdupois. Of course the weight is entirely optional and can be increased to any desired extent to suit individual taste. The sack is then suspended at the height of the karateka's chest.

Fig. 41 illustrates an implement made of stone weighing

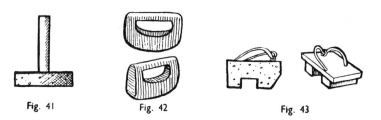

Fig. 41                    Fig. 42                    Fig. 43

about ten pounds avoirdupois. It is technically known as a "chishi". Fig. 42 illustrates two handle-shaped implements made of iron or stone which can be used in much the same way as iron dumb-bells and with much the same efficacy. These are dubbed "sashi". Fig. 43 shows a pair of Japanese-style clogs called geta but made of stone and iron respectively. They are worn by the karateka for the purpose of strengthening and developing all the leg and thigh muscles. Their weight is not given. Figs. 44 and 45 show a jar, the size of which

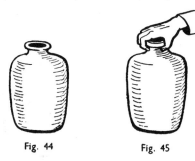

Fig. 44                    Fig. 45

is optional but the shape indicated should be adhered to. It is used as shown in Fig. 45 to strengthen the karateka's grip in which the thumb and finger joints and the palm of the hand play an important part. Fig. 46 describes what in karate parlance is called a "strength stone". It is useful also for strengthening the grip. Two other contrivances not illustrated are (1) the sandbox which may be filled with either peas or sand and whose purpose is to strengthen the karateka's finger-tips which are frequently used to apply lethal thrusts at an opponent's throat, and (2) a sandbag (sunabukuro) to train the fist, elbows, &c. Fig. 47 shows two iron rings about an inch and a half thick and oval in shape measuring about a foot in length. They are to be gripped in order to strengthen

Fig. 46    Fig. 47

the arms and hands. Fig. 48 shows a bar-bell familiar to every athlete. In karate its weight may vary from about 88 lbs. to approximately 176 lbs. It is, of course, lifted with both hands, pressed up and lowered consecutively as often as the karateka's powers of endurance will allow. The dumb-bells shown in Fig. 49 have only recently been introduced in karate

Fig 48    Fig 49

and their use does not call for comment. The same remark applies to Fig. 50, the familiar chest expander.

Fig. 51 however illustrates a karate speciality and therefore calls for rather more detailed examination. It is distinctively dubbed "Kaketebiki", which may be literally translated to mean "to hang and pull with the hand". On much the same lines as the post used for the makiwara part of the post is

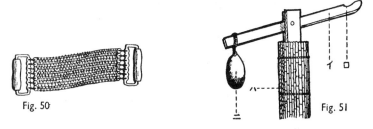

Fig. 50    Fig. 51

fixed in the earth and above the ground a length of about four feet is thickly bound round with slender bamboo or cane strips. About five inches above this casing or about four feet from the surface of the ground a hole is made in the post through which a pole is passed. Both ends can then be operated in the manner of a see-saw. This apparatus serves as a convenient compendium for training in the kakete, hikite, nukite, hijiate, &c. earlier described in these pages. Fig. 52 represents what is somewhat euphemistically called a hairpin made of iron or brass which the karateka brandishes and flourishes in various ways to develop the strength of his wrist.

The zealous young karateka is enjoined to neglect no opportunity of hardening and toughening his hands and feet

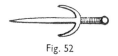

Fig. 52

which are the most important weapons in his natural armory designed for both defence and counter-attack. With the use of the makiwara he should practise daily and as long as he can conveniently do so until eventually he has developed such tremendous power that with a single blow he is able to shatter a bundle of sticks and with a single kick split several boards piled one upon the other.

## Method of Training the Normal Fist (Seiken)

*Preparatory posture:* Take up your position at a convenient distance facing the makiwara so that your outstretched hand can touch the target without your having to lean too far forward. Keep your upper body straight. The blow with your right fist should coincide with a step forward of the left foot and the blow with your left fist with a step forward of your right foot. Both knees should be sufficiently bent and your hips somewhat lowered. As Fig. 53 shows, the back of the striking fist, in this case the right, is held downward at the hip, and the back of the other fist upwards. It is also assumed that you will practise striking the makiwara in the various postures already explained in section III, e.g. zenkutsutachi, kokutsutachi, kibatachi, neko-ashitachi, &c. Next, when thrusting with either right or left fist, as it comes forward you twist it so that just before it strikes the makiwara the back of the fist is turned upwards; then as you withdraw it you again twist it so that when it returns to your hip the back is
36

held downwards. Again, with your fists in front of your knees when you thrust with your left fist your right fist is held at your right hip with the back downwards and when you thrust with your right fist your left fist is held at your left hip with the back downwards. And as you withdraw your right fist your left fist moves forward and as you withdraw your left fist your right fist moves forward and so you revert to your starting posture. The importance is emphasized of early estimating the co-ordination between the thrusting fist and the

Fig. 53

withdrawing hand until gradually you acquire the necessary degree of skill. At first you should thrust several times rather gently at regular intervals and then gradually infuse strength into your blows. In this way if you practise morning and evening and as your skill develops you can increase the number of blows *ad lib*. On the other hand, if at the start you recklessly thrust too strongly and too often you may hurt your fist and therefore be obliged to discontinue practice until the hand gets better. Once your fists have become thoroughly hardened you should be careful not to let them get soft again. Another point to be borne in mind is that if when starting from the hip position you put too much strength into your thrust the bodily action is likely to be blunted and the power of your final thrust lessened. It is preferable lightly to close your fist at the start of the movement from the hip and then immediately before the fist reaches the makiwara suddenly put strength into it. The speed of the withdrawal of your fist to the hip is a little greater than the time of the thrust. On no account should your wrist be bent either up or down when you strike the makiwara. It should be held quite straight. The reason is that if it is at all crooked not only is the power of your striking fist minimized but often you may sprain or injure the fingers. Figs. 54a and 54b illustrate the wrong way of holding the

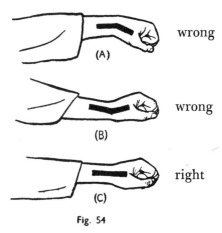

Fig. 54

wrist and fist and Fig. 54c the correct one when striking. It does not always follow that the direction of the back of the fist when thrusting must be upwards. Sometimes, according to circumstances, it may be laterally outwards, obliquely, as when you are dealing an upper cut at your opponent's lower jaw, when the back of the fist is directed towards him. The foregoing data do not exhaust the positions to be practised when training the normal fist (seiken). Thus when running from a distance, retreating together with the thrust or when separated about a foot from the makiwara, i.e. when trying to stretch your arm in the relevant position, you thrust with a jump-in. This sort of training is essential for real fighting but should be essayed only after you have mastered the fundamental thrusting methods already described.

When the head of your fist happens to be painful, then without actually hitting the makiwara you can halt the thrusting fist about an inch or two before it. Lastly two or three things should be noted concerning the height of the fist in relation to the hip. As a rule the fist is held so that the elbow is at right-angles (Fig. 55a). But according to the teacher concerned it can be held just below the breast with the fist and the elbow almost horizontal (Fig. 55b) and the elbow pulled backwards. In Fig. 55c the elbow is only half drawn backwards. The last explanation applies to a posture designed to facilitate striking from close quarters. Again there is the posture depicted in Fig. 55d in which the fist is held above the breast. Although it may be a little too high, since you should practise to strike with the fist in any position, it is advisable to train from the said position concurrently with

Fig. 55 A                              Fig. 55 B

the one illustrated in Fig. 55a with the elbow half-way drawn backwards.

For the tempering of the seiken (normal fist) both the stationary and portable makiwara and the sandbag are utilized. *Inter alia* they serve to harden the head of the fist, to develop the speed of the thrust, to teach the right use of strength, to enable you better to understand the principle of atemi or methods of attacking vital spots, to take up a suitable position and at the right distance from your opponent, to regulate your respiration both when inhaling and exhaling, to cultivate strength of the arms, shoulders, abdomen, &c., and to accustom the arm and shoulder joints to reaction. Essentially there are four kinds of thrusting methods which are briefly described as follows: (1) CHOKUTSUKI *or direct thrust:* This is deemed to be the fundamental one among thrusting methods. It is classified into three divisions, viz., the jodantsuki or upper-step thrust which is aimed at the

39

opponent's face; the chudantsuki or middle-step thrust which is aimed at his chest area, and the gedantsuki or lower-step thrust which is aimed at his abdominal region. (2) AGETSUKI *or rising thrust,* otherwise the upper-cut. In this method you ward off your opponent's attack, grip his attacking hand, pull it towards you and then with your other hand clenched and moving from down upwards hit his lower jaw. (3) FURITSUKI *or swinging thrust:* Swinging your fist to right or left you aim a blow at your opponent's face, flank, &c. (4) WATSUKI *or circle thrust:* When your thrust-out fist is stopped by your

Fig. 55 C      Fig. 55 D

opponent then from that position you describe a complete circle with it and deliver a blow.

At this point our Japanese author resumes his explanation of methods of hand and arm training with the several makiwara to supplement the earlier one confined to the normal fist or seiken. First then is the

HIRAKEN *(flat or level fist):* The same principle is exemplified as when you are striking with the seiken. You take up your position facing the makiwara and train the hiraken by dealing downward slanting blows from above your head or else standing in an oblique lateral position you deal direct blows at the makiwara.

URAKEN *or under side fist:* When training the right or left uraken you stand in an oblique right or left lateral position before the makiwara and bringing your right or left fist to the region of your left or right ear hit the makiwara. Again, standing in front of the makiwara turn the back of the fist from

40

under the jaw towards the makiwara or from above the head (the back of fist turned sideways) hit the makiwara from that position.

KENTSUI or *hammer fist:* You stand before the makiwara in an oblique right or left lateral attitude with the back of the fist turned upwards obliquely above the head, from which position you strike the makiwara. Again, standing right or left obliquely sideways before the makiwara with the back of the right or left fist turned downwards near the left or right ear you strike the makiwara.

NUKITE or *piercing hand:* For the training of the nukite, the makiwara, sandbag and sandbox are all three utilized. When you are training the four-finger nukite the finger-tips must be carefully arranged. When you are using the sandbox, at the start sand is put in and the finger-tips are arranged and thrust in; then peas are used and finally you train them with the makiwara. If one has successfully completed one's training one can easily smash boards or damage an opponent's bones!

TEGATANA or *handsword:* You hit the makiwara from the side obliquely. Two ways are described: (*a*) When you are hardening the right tegatana you assume the so-called kibatachi or equestrian posture obliquely to the right side with the palm held upwards near to the left ear from which position you deliver your blows. When the blow is dealt the palm is uppermost. (*b*) Again you assume the kibatachi posture to the left obliquely with the back of the hand held upwards at the right side of the head from which position you deliver the downward blow. The left tegatana is executed conversely.

EMPI OR HIJIATE: (*a*) TATE-EMPI or *vertical empi:* You stand sideways opposite the makiwara with your fist held in contact with your hip from which the elbow is raised to strike. You may imagine that you deal the blow upwards at the solar-plexus of an enemy who is approaching you from the side to seize your hand. (*b*) SAGETA-EMPI or *lowered empi:* For this method the sandbag is placed on the ground and your elbow is driven downwards to deal the blow. (*c*) ZENEMPI or *frontal empi:* You stand in front of the makiwara and bring your right or left fist up near to your right or left ear, with the little finger edge turned towards the ear. From this posture with your elbow you strike the makiwara as though you were dealing blows at an enemy's chest, solar-plexus, &c. (d) KOEMPI or rear empi: You stand one pace in front of the makiwara with your back turned to it. Your right or left fist is brought near to the side of your right or left ear, the back of the fist turned upwards. From this posture you should with lightning speed draw your elbow to the rear to deal the blow. Moreover according to the same principle, from the jodantsuki and chudantsuki positions the fist in contact with the hip, as you turn the fist you draw the elbow backwards and strike the makiwara. (e) YOKO-EMPI or lateral empi: The same as when training the tate-empi you stand before the makiwara turned to the side, the back of your right or left fist turned downwards. After bringing it near to your left or right shoulder you strike the makiwara as though you were attacking an enemy's solar-plexus. At the moment of the blow the fist and elbow are horizontal in front of your chest. (f) HINERI-YOKO-EMPI or twisting-lateral-empi: You stand in front of the makiwara with the thumb-edge of your left and right fists near to both breasts and the elbows extended. Then taking a pace forward, hips lowered, you strike with both right and left elbows. At this moment you must be particularly careful not to let the upper part of your body fall forward with your shoulders stretched.

UKETE (defence hand) and wrist: When training the ukete you should not bend the wrist but keep it outstretched. (a) OMOTETEKUBI or outside wrist: You stand obliquely to the right or left side of the makiwara. The back of your right or left fist is turned upwards, the left or right side of the body well withdrawn. As you turn the back of your fist the thumb edge of your wrist hits the makiwara. Again you stand obliquely to the left or right side of the makiwara, the back of your right or left fist to the side. After receding to the right or left side you strike the makiwara. (b) URATEKUBI or back wrist: You stand obliquely to the right or left-hand side of the makiwara. The back of your right or left fist is lowered and having withdrawn the back of the fist to the right or left side of the body you strike the makiwara. (c) URATEKUBI or back wrist: You stand obliquely on the right or left side of the makiwara. The back of your right or left fist is lowered, and after you have receded to the right or left side and as you turn the back of your fist upwards you strike the makiwara with the little finger edge of the wrist. (*d*) HIRATEKUBI or *flat (ordinary) wrist.* As in the previous two cases you stand obliquely to the right or left side of the makiwara. The back of your right or left fist is turned downwards. The left or right side of your body is withdrawn and as you turn the back of your fist sideways, i.e., in the direction of the makiwara, you strike it. MYAKUHAKUGAWA-TEKUBI *or pulsation side of wrist:* When your thrust forward fist is parried with your opponent's forearm, the under side of your flat wrist (the pulsation side) crashes into his forearm. In order to be prepared for such an eventuality and to reduce the impetus of this action you harden the underside of the flat wrist. Thus you stand obliquely to the left or right side of the makiwara with the right or left fist raised to the right or left side, and after stretching it forward you strike the makiwara with the pulsation side of it.

METHODS OF TEMPERING THE KAMIASHIZOKO OR BOTTOM OF UPPER PART OF FOOT: In the karate repertoire methods of kicking (keriwaza) naturally play a very important role. It is therefore imperative that in order to develop great kicking strength training of the normal feet should not be overlooked. Seeing that the sole of the foot is utilized in the technique styled footsword (ashigatana) in contra-distinction to the handsword (tegatana), the importance of adequate training will be apparent. This training with the makiwara must be done from the various postures already listed, e.g. fudotachi (immobile posture), nekoashitachi (cat's foot posture), zenkutsutachi (inclined posture), &c. You stand in front of the makiwara with the back of both fists held downwards in contact with both hips. In the case of the fudotachi posture the back foot and in the case of the nekoashitachi posture the front foot is used to kick the makiwara. After giving the kick you must swiftly bring back the foot to its original position.

METHODS OF TEMPERING THE SHIMOASHIZOKO OR BOTTOM OF THE LOWER PART OF THE FOOT: These correspond to those of the kamiashizoko (upper part of the foot) just described.

METHODS OF TEMPERING THE ASHIGATANA OR FOOTSWORD: You stand obliquely to the right or left side or in front of the makiwara and kick it with either foot in a lateral direction.

Taking the various appliances already described elsewhere in their proper sequence you begin with that shown in Fig. 41, known as the chishi. You grip the haft as you stand in the shikotachi or four-thigh-posture and using left and right hand alternately carry out the following eight exercises: (1) With the elbow raised you first lower the stone or iron implement and then radiating as it were from your shoulders whirl it round several times. (2) You lift the chishi several times. Then with your arm held a little lower than the height of the shoulder you extend it in a direct line several times. (3) Holding the chishi upright you bend your arm sideways several times. (4) Lifting the chishi and holding your hand at shoulder level with the chishi stretched out, you gently lower and raise it several times. (5) With your hand outstretched and your elbow moving in a bent position you whirl the chishi outwards and obliquely sideways and downwards to the front, and repeat the action several times. (6) On the same principle as the foregoing but in this case the whirling movement is inwards, obliquely sideways and downwards to the front. Repeat several times. (7) With both hands grasping the haft of the chishi you describe an arc from up downwards and then in the opposite direction from down upwards, and repeat several times the action of raising and lowering the chishi outwards. (8) In this case the movements are done inwards. You hold the chishi close to your jaw and chest and several times repeat the action of raising and lowering.

The next apparatus is called the sashi (see Fig. 42) which may be likened to handles made of iron. You grip them with both hands and holding them in this manner bend and stretch your arms up and down and from left to right.

Next the iron or stone geta (Japanese clogs, see Fig. 43) which are worn to strengthen the leg muscles. Their efficacy is increased when you use them in conjunction with the sashi described above. You raise the sashi with both hands and from inwards outwards while describing a semi-circle and walk to and fro until you feel you have had enough.

Next the jar or kame (see Figs. 44 and 45). This at first you lift empty with both hands and move quietly forward

44

in a semi-circular direction. Then gradually the weight of the jar can be increased by filling it with sand, then gravel, rock and even lead in that sequence. This method is employed to strengthen the hips and loins, the arms and shoulders and the karateka's grip.

The next appliance is the so-called chikara-ishi or "strength stone" (see Fig. 46). You grip it with your left and right hand alternately and develop strength by repeatedly lifting and lowering it.

The appliances illustrated in Figs. 47, 48, 49 and 50 do not call for additional description, but inasmuch as the so-called kaketebiki shown in Fig. 51 is a highly important and distinctive accessory of karate our Japanese author has at this stage devoted considerable space to an explanation of its application to the special needs of defence and counterattack. Thus the kaketebiki facilitates your training to ward

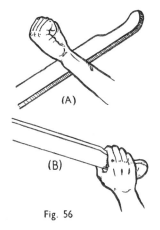

Fig. 56

off an opponent's attacking hand with your own wrist or forearm, simultaneously to grip his hand and as you pull and overthrow him kick his knee-joint, his ribs, apply an empi technique, nukite, &c. In further detail: The wooden arm of the apparatus marked $\mathsf{T}$ (Fig. 51) is used to train yourself in the kakete, hikite and empi methods. The wooden arm of the apparatus is supposed to represent the opponent's arm. You defend yourself with the manoeuvre depicted in Fig. 56a which is called the omotekubi or outer wrist. At this stage you can hold your defence hand in the tegatana (handsword) or seiken (normal fist) style with the back turned outwards. Next with the hand which has made the defence you reverse your palm and grasping the wooden arm, as shown in Fig. 56b, pull it downwards. Reference to Fig. 51 will show that a heavy sandbag is suspended from the opposite end of the wooden arm marked ⚌ to afford some resistance to this action. Afterwards concurrently with the action of your pulling hand you violently kick the spot marked /\ in Fig. 51 which consists of a bundle of bamboo sticks enclosing the post of the kaketebiki. And you also strike the same spot with your left and right elbow. Then to toughen your fingers for the nukite or piercing hand you thrust them repeatedly among the bamboo sticks. The kaketebiki equally serves for purposes of lateral defence by toughening the forearm and wrist against the wooden arm. If your forearm and wrist have been well tempered by both the kaketebiki and the makiwara, when your opponent attacks you with his hands or feet you ought to be able not only to ward off his assault but deal him such a counter-blow as to render him incapable of renewing it. In this manner the intrinsic value of karate alike in defence and counter-attack is clearly exemplified. Our Japanese author goes on to describe the various ways in which a rope can be utilized in the karateka's training, e.g. skipping, jumping, climbing, &c. Seeing that most Western athletes are familiar with all of them detailed recapitulation here would be redundant. The same remark applies to the well-known exercise usually called "on the hands down" much in favor in both Japanese and western dojo for the purpose of developing the arms and shoulders. For cultivation of power in the shoulders, hips, loins, waist and legs use is made of the portable makiwara depicted in Figs. 40a and 40b. Thus the flat of the hand can be applied to push it away or it can be kicked *ad lib*. You should learn to approach it from various positions. From the context it would seem that the portable makiwara used for this purpose is the type suspended at about the height of the chest so that you can practise the various parries and blows, especially the elbow blows or hijiate dealt in the zenempi or frontal empi styles.

Instead of using the portable makiwara two players whom we may call respectively A and B go through a series of movements the karate name of which, To-jin-ho, means literally "the falling person method". A and B take their stand facing each other. A adopts a cautionary attitude. B stands in a slight zenkutsutachi posture with both elbows held lightly against the body and both hands opened in front. He is leaning forward bent at the hips in the shape of the Japanese character <. Then A, keeping his body upright, falls down in front of B. Then infusing strength into his lower abdomen (saika tanden), B from his bent position supports A. B bends his upper body backwards, then slowly straightens it, stretches out both hands and restores A to his former posture. In the execution of these movements the distance between the performers must not be exceeded. Again A and B confront each other and execute the movement several times. By degrees and as the strength of hips and loins is developed A puts more and more power into his action and ends by running towards B and then falling.

The next movement called Hanten-ho means literally "to turn from side to side" and is a variation of the To-jin-ho just described. In this case A extends both hands and measures the distance by placing them on B's shoulders. Then both of them assume the zenkutsutachi posture and A with the palms of both hands pushes against B's shoulders but this time strength is imparted to the action. The reason for this is that if strength were not imparted then only with the hand would A repel B with no response from the body, so that strength in the loins and hips would not be cultivated. The moment A pushes B and just before his hands touch B's shoulders, B thrusts A's forearms upwards to repulse the attack. There are two ways of doing this, as follows:

(a) MIGIHANTEN *(right hanten):* B opposes a right tegatana to A's left outer forearm (the left-hand thumb edge) and applies his left palm to A's right under forearm (the right hand little finger edge). If B succeeds in parrying deeply, that is as close as possible to both A's forearms, and elbows, it will be easy to break his balance. The direction of propulsion is obliquely right from below upwards with both hands. If the push were not obliquely upwards then A's hand might strike B's own face.

(b) HIDARIHANTEN *(left hanten):* B opposes a left tegatana to A's right under forearm and applies his right palm to A's left under forearm. Then on left and right he simultaneously pushes upwards in a left oblique direction. The practice closes when A pushes with both hands and B thrusts them aside with a left and right tegatana from inside outwards and blocks both A's forearms.

We now come to what are termed the "Seven-step-kick-training" (Shichidan-keri-no-renshuho), as follows: These are important and should be described in series.

No. 1 Dan: The attacker is supposed to thrust upwards with his kneecap against his opponent's abdominal region and scrotum.

No. 2 Dan: The attacker in this movement is supposed to kick his opponent's scrotum with his ankle.

No. 3 Dan: In this case the kick to the opponent's scrotum is delivered with the upper part of the sole.

No. 4 Dan: The kick to the opponent's lower abdomen is dealt with the lower part of the sole.

No. 5 Dan: Assuming that you are hugged from behind by your opponent you step back and stamp heavily upon his instep.

No. 6 Dan: From the No. 5 Dan position but this time using your back heel you kick upwards at your assailant's scrotum.

No. 7 Dan: The ashigatana (footsword) is used to deal a kick at your opponent's knee-joint. The direction of the kick is obliquely frontal.

When practising the No. 7 Dan kick you should imagine that you are confronting a living opponent. From No. 1 Dan to No. 7 Dan you should once at least keep one foot off the ground and successively execute the movements at high speed. And other than when transferring from No. 5 Dan to No. 6 Dan, as a general rule the feet should be returned to their original position, raised and with the knees deeply bent. Both hands should be clenched and held at the hips or the palms so held. When the palms are at the hips the fingers are extended. The upper part of the body is not erect and your weight is imposed on one leg.

**Thrust Kick to kneecap and . . .**

**Roundhouse Kick to the head.**

A

**In the Head Grasp . . .**

B

draw your
opponent's head
down as . . .

you raise your
knee to meet it.

C

**A Low Block against an attempted kick to the groin.**

D

**Thrust Kick countered by Outside Forearm Block.**

E

**Sidethrust Kick to armpit.**

High Kick to chin.

Inside Forearm Block.

G

**Knifehand Block against a punch to the head.**

H

**Knifehand Block, countering with elbow in a Horse Stance.**

I

**Thrust Kick from floor to ribs.**

J

## CHAPTER VI

### FUNDAMENTAL TRAINING METHODS—PRELIMINARY KATA

EXIGENCIES of space necessitate considerable condensation of the Japanese author's introductory remarks about the katas or forms which the karate student is expected to learn before attempting the final so-called kumite kata or forms of contest practised by two performers. Nor would any useful purpose be served by overburdening this section with all the technical terms contained in the copious karate vocabulary to describe the several methods of training. The two main divisions seem to be the Renzoku-Renshuho (successive or consecutive training method) and the Renketsu-Renshuho (coupling or linking method). The former teaches the manner of advancing, retreating and moving sideways and the latter is designed to couple or link all these methods. The Renzoku-Renshuho comprises the so-called Shinko Kata (advance or progress kata) in which we also find the Chokusen Kata (straight line kata) and the Hasen Kata (wave line kata). In Fig. 57 the line marked "a" represents the straight line kata and the line marked "b" the wave line kata. The following is a description of the straight line kata:

1. CHUDANTSUKI (*literally "middle-step thrust"*, i.e. blows at the opponent's middle body): These movements are described as the most important of the fundamental ones and the student is therefore urged to repeat them until mastery has been achieved.

*Principle:* CHUDAN-RENZOKU-OITSUKI *(middle-step-successive-pursuit thrust):* At the word of command you assume the outer hachijitachi posture and from this the left zenkutsu-tachi posture, i.e. the preparatory posture shown in Fig. 58 and from that to the one shown in Fig. 59 where your left foot is advanced and your right foot drawn back a pace. At the same time your right hand is held obliquely left downwards with the palm open and pointing upwards. Your left hand is held in front of your left shoulder with the palm open and directed upwards. With the sensation of what is rather vaguely

49

called a reciprocally withdrawing stretching reaction your right fist (just before strongly clenched in the seiken or normal fist style against the hip) is held with the back turned downwards towards the right hip and your left hand held as though in readiness to repel an attack with hand or leg from the front. Your little finger edge forearm is held strongly in the gedan-uke position to repel an attack against the lower part of your body and the hand is closed in the seiken (normal fist) style. Your posture now is the left zenkutsutachi with the

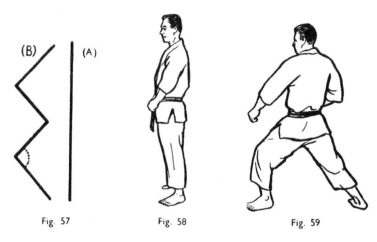

Fig. 57          Fig. 58          Fig. 59

left fist about six or seven inches above the left knee. The general posture is one in which the hips are lowered, the upper part of the body held upright and the chest expanded It is directed diagonally right, the feet to the front, strength infused into the lower abdomen and stability well preserved The face is turned to the front (the chudantsuki style), the eyes are widely opened and gaze as it were into the face of an imaginary opponent.

Next at the word of command "Hajime!" (begin) you assume the posture depicted in Fig. 60 with your right foot planted a good pace in front of your left foot, i.e. in the right zenkutsutachi posture. Simultaneously your left fist is held firmly against your left hip and above your left knee and in readiness as though to grasp an opponent's attacking hand leg, &c. and pull it towards you. Your right fist is extended with the back twisted upwards and your gaze is fixed on an

50

imaginary opponent in front of you preparatory to thrusting at the area of his solar-plexus. Your advanced foot should be allowed to slide lightly over the surface of the ground with the strength taken out of it and must never be lifted too high. The advance of your foot and the blow with your fist must not be simultaneous. The advanced foot is planted on the ground just before the blow is struck. If this line of demarcation is drawn between the two movements the power of the striking fist is increased. On the other hand the projection of the striking fist and the withdrawal of the other fist to your hip are simultaneous. On no account must there be any incongruity

Fig. 60

between the movements involved, i.e. both should be equally swift and not one swift and the other slow. The reason is that should the fist dealing the blow be eluded by your opponent, and while your own posture is broken many opportunities are afforded your opponent to take advantage of such maladjustment before you can regain your balanced posture. If the thrust and withdrawal are effected simultaneously then even if your first attack has failed and your opponent has escaped you may be able to stage a second defence. Moreover if you strike your opponent with a tenth unit of power then the withdrawn fist should be carried to the hip with a twelfth unit of power. The posture at the time of the thrust is with the shoulders lowered, not stretched, the wrist not bent upwards or downwards or to left or right, and the top of the fist held in a straight line from the shoulder. The upper part of your body is held upright confronting an imaginary opponent and

51

must not protrude when the blow is struck. Your face should be directed to the front as though you were gazing into the eyes of your opponent. And of course when there is a real opponent you will look at his eyes. According to the foregoing principle, consecutively right and left while advancing you train in the style termed Chudan-Renzoku-Oitsuki (middle-step-successive-pursuit-thrust).

In the case of the Chudan-Renzoku-Gyakutsuki (middle-step-successive-reverse-thrust) when the word of command is given to prepare for this kata you assume the outer hachijitachi posture and then, as for the oitsuki, the left zenkutsutachi posture in preparation for the left gedan-uke [lower step (body) defence] and after first standing with your right fist in contact with your right hip, from that position, as shown in Fig. 61, you raise your right fist for the chudantsuki or middle body thrust

Fig. 61                                              Fig. 62

when your left fist is brought in contact with your left hip. This is the preparatory posture. When the word of command "Hajime!" (begin) is given you take a step forward with your right foot and your left fist is raised for the chudantsuki and your right fist is brought to your right hip. The advance in this style constitutes the chudan-renzoku-gyakutsuki; viz., as regards the oitsuki, when your left or right foot is advanced to the front you strike with your left or right fist, but as regards the gyakutsuki your left or right foot is advanced and you are striking with your right or left fist. The reason why this movement is called the gyakutsuki is that the movements of the hands and legs are contrary to each other. In this way you

52

train in the shikotachi, kibatachi, &c. for the jodan, chudan and gedan attacks, alternately with left and right hand as many as a hundred or two hundred times. This training is mainly for the purpose of cultivating staying power.

2. JODANTSUKI: In this style you are supposed to be attacking your opponent's face. The principle is identical with that of the chudantsuki. Only for the jodantsuki you attack your opponent's face, the middle of the forehead, the jinchu or vital spot beneath the nose, the jaw, &c.

3. GEDANTSUKI: In this style your attack is directed against your opponent's abdominal area, scrotum, &c. Or when your opponent essays to kick your scrotum, solar-plexus, lower abdomen, &c., with your hand you grasp his shin and thrust it down. The principle is identical with the chudantsuki.

4. WAY OF TURNING RIGHT OR LEFT: If when executing the aforesaid jodantsuki, chudantsuki and gedantsuki and while continuously thrusting with left and right fist alternately an obstacle should obtrude, then your further advance may be prevented. In that case you utter the kiai shout and move round to right or left to deal the last blow.

*Principle:* In the case of the oitsuki (pursuit thrust), for example, when you are standing in the left zenkutsutachi posture the turning movement to the right is executed as follows: With the left heel as axis you describe a turn of 180 degrees pointing in the direction of your former advance and take up the right zenkutsutachi posture. Your right fist is held in the gedan-uke style, the space between the fist and knee-cap being about six or seven inches, and your left fist is at your left hip. Whilst rotating you adopt the gedan-uke posture as though to ward off a kick from the rear. The ensuing advance method is as already stated. As regards the principle involved when doing a left turn in the case of the right zenkutsutachi posture, the left zenkutsutachi posture is the exact opposite. In the case of the gyakutsuki, to make a right turn in the right zenkutsu-tachi posture, according to the same principle as when doing a right turn for the oitsuki, you assume the right zenkutsutachi posture and together with the right fist when executing the gedan-uke, your left fist is brought to your left hip. Next, the right fist, which has carried out the gedan-uke, is drawn to the right hip and at the same time is thrust to the front. While you

53

are holding the right zenkutsutachi posture, when you make a left turn the movement is the reverse of the left zenkutsutachi posture and a right turn.

5. GEDAN-UKE *(lower step defence):* From the outer hachijitachi posture you take a pace to the rear and assume the left zenkutsutachi posture. With your left fist you execute the gedan-uke and bring your right fist to your right hip. While executing this gedan-uke left and right alternately you advance. If advance becomes impossible then in the last defensive position you utter the kiai shout and retreat.

6. CHUDAN-TEGATANA-UKE *(defence with the middle-step handsword):* When the opponent attacks your chest area you defend yourself with the tegatana which is supposed to deal the attacking hand or leg a crushing blow.

*Principle:* In preparation for the chudan-renzoku-tegatana-uke you adopt the outer hachijitachi posture and from that position retract your right foot to the rear to take up the nekoashitachi posture and as your right hand forms a tegatana in front of your chest and your left hand forms a tegatana starting from the front of your right shoulder, back of hand turned downwards, the elbow half bent, you confront an imaginary opponent and deal a sweeping blow at his middle body (chudan) (Fig. 62). When your left hand is withdrawn to your right shoulder the back of the hand is turned downwards, but just before the sweeping blow is dealt at the imaginary enemy's hand or foot, the hand is turned so that its back points obliquely upwards. The finger-tips of the tegatana are generally at the height of the shoulder.

At the word of command "Hajime!" (begin) you step forward with your right foot in front of your left foot and adopt the nekoashitachi posture and while at the same time you make a left tegatana in front of your chest you make a right tegatana in the chudan-uke style. You repeat this action alternately right and left while advancing. If you cannot advance then in the last defensive position you utter the kiai shout and retreat.

7. JODAN-AGE-UKE *(upper step-lift-defence):* When your opponent aims a blow at your upper body you defend yourself by raising up his attacking hand from below.

*Principle:* From the outer hachijitachi posture, at the word of command for the jodan-renzoku-age-uke preparatory

54

posture, as shown in Fig. 63, your right foot is withdrawn a pace so that you adopt the left fudotachi posture and at the same time your right fist is brought to your right hip and the back of your left fist is turned inwards, i.e. with the little finger edge upwards, and sweeps upwards above your forehead.

At the start you step forward with your right foot in front of your left foot and adopt the right fudotachi posture, and at the same time as you withdraw your left fist to your left hip, with your right fist you sweep upwards above your forehead.

Fig. 63                    Fig. 64

When executing the jodan-age-uke you ward off the opponent's attacking hand with your under forearm (which one not stated) from below upwards. Your upper body must not be bent backwards or inclined forward. In accordance with this principle you advance while alternately practising the jodan-age-uke left and right. If advance cannot be made then at the last defensive position you utter the kiai shout and retreat.

8.   JODAN-UCHI-KOMI *(upper step-drive or strike-in)*: You are attacking your imaginary opponent's face or shoulder area with a kentsui (hammer fist) or assuming that your opponent strikes at your upper body you retort with a kentsui, your wrist, &c. and powerfully strike down his attacking hand.

*Principle:* At the word of command for preparation for the jodan-renzoku-uchi-komi (upper step-successive-strike-in), from the outer hachijitachi posture (Fig. 64) you draw back your right foot a step and adopt a right kokutsutachi posture (retroflex posture) with your right fist against your right hip, while with your left fist held above your head, the little finger edge directed upwards, you instantly deal a downright blow in front of the eyes in a somewhat diagonal direction. At the moment of the blow the back of the left fist is turned obliquely downwards.

At the word of command "Hajime!" (begin) you step forward a pace with your right foot in front of your left foot to assume the left kokutsutachi posture. Your left fist is at your left hip and with your right fist you deal the jodan-uchi-komi blow. According to this principle you execute the movement left and right as you advance and when you cannot advance at the moment of the last uchi-komi or strike-in you utter the kiai shout and retreat. This movement is not illustrated.

9. KERI-KOMI *(kick-in):* This method has already been described in the section on ashiwaza or foot and leg techniques, but the Japanese author adds here a paragraph on the method of training for the renzoku-keri-komi or successive kick-in. At the word of command to get ready you adopt the outer hachijitachi posture and from this posture you pass to the left zenkutsutachi posture, as shown in Fig. 65, with both

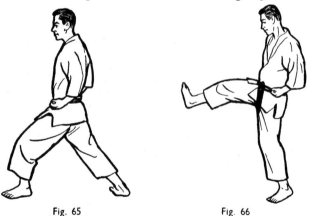

Fig. 65                    Fig. 66

your fists against your hips, their backs turned downwards. At the word of command to begin, as shown in Fig. 66, you kick to the front with the sole of your right foot and then instantly withdraw the foot to its original position when the thigh and shin are perpendicular. You step forward as shown in Figs. 67

56

and 68. When you kick with your right foot the knee of your left leg is slightly bent and the leg supports your body, and when you kick with your left foot the knee of your right leg is slightly bent and the leg supports your body. At all times both your fists are placed at your hips and when you kick you practise to do so as strongly and as high as possible. In an actual fight, however, should you kick too high your posture might be broken and so weakened. Since your adversary might be quick to take advantage of such a situation you are advised to exercise caution so as to avert that danger.

Fig. 67                              Fig. 68

According to the foregoing principle you advance while kicking alternately left and right.

*Right turn:* According to the same principle, as exemplified in the frontal kick, when doing a right turn you continue to advance while kicking. Only both your hands are held at your hips as you rotate.

10. YOKOGERI *(lateral kick):* This method can be practised in two ways, viz,. with the ashigatana or with the sole of the foot, but the explanation given below applies to the ashigatana method.

*Principle:* At the word of command to get ready for the renzoku ashigatana or successive footsword kick, you adopt the outer hachijitachi posture in a right lateral kicking direction. Both hands are closed in the seiken or normal fist style with their backs turned downwards at both hips, or the palms held with the thumbs at the side of the forefingers can be applied to the hips.

At the word of command to begin you stand as shown in Fig. 69 with your left leg passed a step in front of your right leg. As shown in Fig. 70, while your right foot is raised you kick with an ashigatana direct sideways at an imaginary opponent's sides and abdomen; then the foot is withdrawn and slightly lowered and you take up the outer hachijitachi posture. Concurrently for a second time, after advancing your left foot a pace sideways across your right leg you kick to the side with an ashigatana. When kicking you must not bend your upper body but keep it upright. For the lateral kick you

Fig. 69                                    Fig. 70

do not make a right or left turn, i.e. while kicking with a right ashigatana you advance sideways and when your advance is forced to stop, retaining that posture, at the word of command to begin in the opposite direction you take a step to the side with your right foot from in front of your left foot and deliver a left lateral ashigatana kick. Thereafter you repeatedly practise these movements as you advance sideways.

We are told that there are many more successive training methods than those already described but at this stage the latter will suffice. These successive training methods coincident with the thrust (tsuki), defence (uke) and the kick (keri) are designed to cultivate the stance or standing posture or staying power and the great importance is emphasized of striving from the first to train seriously so that as you become skilful you can execute all such movements with speed and assurance. Moreover not only must you practise the move-

58

ments in a straight line for advance and retreat but also in the wave-like or undulating line. And if you master the straight line then you ought naturally to be able to understand the principle of the wave-like kata.

In what is called the renketsu renshuho (coupling, linking method of training), e.g. coincident with the chudantsuki or middle-step thrust or blow you can advance with your fist ready for a gedanbarai or lower body sweeping blow, starting off alternately from left and right foot. And when doing the jodan-age-uke or upper-step-lift-defence in order to deliver a gedan-tegatana-barai or sweeping lower body handsword blow, changing the postures while advancing and retreating, with left and right leg alternately you couple the two foregoing techniques in the method of training.

# CHAPTER VII

## KARATE KATA—DAI NIHON KARATE-DO TEN-NO-KATA— TAIKYOKU KATA—PINAN KATA

SEEING that in karate, unlike judo, very few methods can be safely demonstrated to their logical conclusion without the risk of seriously injuring an opponent and must therefore be halted a split second before reaching their target, special importance is naturally ascribed to the study and practice of the relevant karate kata or forms. It should be added that obviously, when a kata is being demonstrated by only one karateka, the risk of injury is no longer involved. It must be admitted that when compared with the judo kata the karate kata tend to appear monotonous and lacking in the latter's spectacular appeal and dynamism. Nonetheless within their own ambit and as an ideal empirical means to an end, i.e. the speediest possible obliteration of a potential enemy, the karate kata cannot fail to impress an intelligent objective observer. And the deeper one delves into the technical details of these forms the less conscious one becomes of the initial impression of their monotony. The so-called kumite kata or contest forms, to which a special section is devoted in these pages, represent perhaps the closest approach to any judo forms. In this section I have confined myself to a description of the most important karate kata, viz., the hyperbolically styled Dai Nihon Karate-Do Ten-no-Kata (literally, Great Japan Karate-Way Heavenly Kata) devised by the celebrated karate teacher Funakoshi, comprising ten movements; the Taikyoku Kata Shodan (a name difficult to translate but perhaps best rendered as the Essential Karate Kata First Step) and the so-called Pinan Shodan, Nidan, Sandan, Yodan and Godan—First Step to Fifth Step—exemplifying in all some 135 movements of which twenty pertain to the Taikyoku Shodan. The following is a description of the Dai Nihon Karate-Do Ten-no-Kata.

In the performance of these kata a very strict etiquette is observed. Thus in Japan it is customary when a formal demonstration is being given for the performer or performers to salute standing, first the shrine of the kami or god and then the shihan or master presiding on the occasion. The method of salutation is as follows: You assume the posture called heisokutachi or blocked feet posture, both hands opened and held naturally in contact with the thighs, your upper body slightly inclined (Fig. 71).

OMOTE-NO-1 : CHUDANOITSUKI *(Outside No. 1, Middle Step Pursuit Thrust)*

*Preparation:* You assume the outer hachijitachi posture, i.e. from the heisokutachi posture you project your left foot and then your right foot to take up the outer hachijitachi posture. The space between your left and right toes is about

Fig. 71          Fig. 72 A          Fig. 72 B

one foot five inches. Your shoulders are lowered and both your fists lightly stretched in front of your thighs. And of course strength should be infused into your lower abdomen while your gaze is fixed on an imaginary opponent in front of you (Figs. 72a and 72b).

(1) You take a big step forward with your right foot and assume the right zenkutsutachi posture while with your right fist you deal a blow at the frontal middle body (chudan) of an imaginary opponent and withdraw your left fist to your left hip (Fig. 73). The instant your right fist has completed its thrust you utter the kiai shout. The forward thrust with your right fist is of course made after your left fist has been withdrawn to your left hip. (This instruction would seem to conflict with the earlier description which implies that the

61

two movements are synchronized.) Your posture at the time of the thrust is with your upper body inclined but your right shoulder must not be pushed forward. Too much strength ought not to be infused into the foot (right) which has stepped forward and your weight is imposed on both legs. Strength is concentrated in your lower abdomen. When you step forward your foot is not raised from the floor but moved along as though pressing the floor from under it.

(2) As you withdraw your right foot to its former position both your fists are lowered and you take up your preparatory

Fig. 73

posture. Although this action is done slowly spirit (ki) is never withdrawn from it.

(3) The reverse of (1).

(4) The reverse of (2).

The above four movements are twice executed after which you pass on to the next kata to which the same principle applies.

OMOTO-NO-2: JODANOITSUKI (*Outside No. 2, Upper Step Pursuit Thrust*)

(1) From the preparatory posture you take a big step forward and assume the right zenkutsutachi posture. At the same time, while you withdraw your left fist to your left hip, with your right fist you deal a blow at the face of an imaginary opponent (Fig. 74). As your fist reaches its supposed mark you utter the kiai shout. It often happens that when executing the jodantsuki your shoulder projects and your posture is broken or when the blow is delivered with your right fist it

62

fails to hit the mark which is supposed to be the center line of your opponent's face, and swerves to the right, counting from yourself. Care should be taken to thrust at the center.

(2)   As you withdraw your right foot to its former position

Fig. 74

you lower both fists and revert to the preparatory posture.

(3)   The reverse of (1).

(4)   The reverse of (2).

OMOTO-NO-3: CHUDANGYAKUTSUKI *(Outside No. 3, Middle Step Reverse Thrust)*

Fig. 75

(1)   You start from the preparatory posture with a forward step of your left foot to assume the left fudotachi posture. Having brought your right fist to your right hip and while your left fist is at your left hip you raise your right fist and

63

thrust it forward in a frontal chudantsuki or middle body blow (Fig. 75). At the instant of the thrust you utter the kiai shout. An important point in connection with the fudotachi posture is that when you step forward with the left foot, although your lower body is turned to the diagonal right, your upper body is really turned to the front and your hips are sufficiently lowered. (Our Japanese author is responsible for this description of a physical feat which only a human body endowed with ambivalence could possibly achieve!)

(2) Your left foot is withdrawn, both your fists are lowered and you revert to the preparatory posture.

(3) The reverse of (1).

(4) The reverse of (2).

Omoto-no-4: Jodangyakutsuki *(Outside No. 4, Upper Step Reverse Thrust)*

(1) With your left foot you take a big pace forward and assume the left fudotachi posture. Having once placed your

Fig. 76

right fist at your right hip and while your left fist is withdrawn to your left hip you raise your right fist and thrust it upwards against an imaginary opponent's upper body (Fig. 76). The instant your fist reaches its supposed target you utter the kiai shout.

(2) As you bring back your left foot to its former position you lower both fists and revert to the preparatory posture.

(3) The reverse of (1).

(4) The reverse of (2).

OMOTE-NO-5: GEDANBARAI-CHUDANTSUKI *(Outside No. 5, Lower Step Sweep-Middle Step Thrust)*

(1)  You take a pace backwards with your right foot to assume the left fudotachi posture. Your right fist is held at your right hip. Your left fist starting from your right shoulder, the back turned downwards, deals a diagonal downward blow about six or seven inches above your left knee-cap. Your upper body assumes what the author calls a half-length posture and the back of your fist is turned upwards. Thus you sweep with your back forearm (Fig. 77).

Fig. 77

(2)  While your left fist is withdrawn to your left hip your right fist makes a frontal chudan (middle step or body) blow. Your feet stay as they are. The instant your fist is thrust forward you utter the kiai shout.

(3)  Your right foot is slowly brought back to its former position, your fists are lowered and you revert to the preparatory posture.

(4)  The reverse of (1).

(5)  The reverse of (2).

(6)  The reverse of (3).

Originally the defence and attack are executed at the same time (sic), i.e. at the instant of the defence you are striking at your opponent but while you are unaccustomed to these movements they may be regarded as two and separately practised. But when you become proficient it is well to practise them as one.

OMOTE-NO-6: CHUDAN-UDE-UKE-CHUDANTSUKI *(Outside 6, Middle Step-Arm-Defence—Middle Step-Thrust)*

(1) From the preparatory posture with your right foot you take a step to the rear and adopt the left fudotachi posture. Your right fist is held against your right hip. With your left fist starting from the right shoulder, the back turned upwards, the elbow half bent and serving as the center, you describe an arc and deal a sweeping blow at an imaginary opponent's middle body (chudan) area (Fig. 78). The sweeping blow is

Fig. 78

dealt as though with the outer wrist (the thumb edge) at the opponent's chest area. The fist is held at the height of the shoulder with the back turned downwards.

(2) Your feet in the same position, your left fist is drawn to your left hip and as with your right fist you deliver a middle body (chudan) blow you utter the kiai shout.

(3) You slowly withdraw your feet to their former position, lower both fists and resume the preparatory posture.

(4) The reverse of (1).

(5) The reverse of (2).

(6) The reverse of (3).

OMOTE-NO-7: CHUDAN-TEGATANA-UKE-CHUDAN-NUKITE *(Outside No. 7, Middle Step-Handsword-Defence—Middle Step-Piercing Hand)*

(1) Withdrawing your right foot a pace to the rear you assume the right kokutsutachi posture. Your right fist is held against your right hip. Preparatory to a tegatana your left hand starts from your right shoulder, the back turned down-

wards, the elbow half bent and the blow is dealt with a sweeping action when the back of the hand is turned obliquely upwards (Fig. 79).

(2) Here you stand with your legs in much the same position. But in this case your left hand clenched is held at your left hip while your right hand is opened to deal a lengthwise nukite at the frontal middle area of an imaginary opponent (Fig. 80). At the instant of the blow you utter the kiai shout. At the time of the nukite your shoulders should

Fig. 79                    Fig. 80

not be raised but sufficiently lowered and strength infused into the armpits.

(3) Your right leg is brought back to its former position. Both your hands are lowered and you revert to the preparatory posture.

(4) The reverse of (1).

(5) The reverse of (2).

(6) The reverse of (3).

OMOTE-NO-8: JODAN-TEGATANABARAI-JODANTSUKI (*Outside No. 8, Upper Step-Handsword-Sweep—Upper Step-Thrust*)

(1) From the preparatory posture you withdraw your right foot a pace to the rear to assume the left fudotachi posture. Your right fist is held against your right hip and your left arm is raised in preparation for a tegatana, the elbow half bent. With the elbow as center you describe an arc as though to ward off an attack and at the height of the eyes deal a sweeping blow. The palm is turned to the front (Fig. 81).

(2) With your feet in the same position and as your left

hand is clenched and held at your left hip, with your right fist you strike at the upper part (jodan) of an imaginary opponent. The delivery of the blow coincides with your utterance of the kiai shout. The sense of the author's clumsily worded note seems to be that when you have warded off with a left tegatana your opponent's attack you seize his wrist and pull him towards your left hip and having thus broken his posture or balance, strike at his upper body with your right fist.

Fig. 81

(3) You bring back your right foot to its former position, lower both fists and resume the preparatory posture.

(4) The exact reverse of (1).

(5) The exact reverse of (2).

(6) The exact reverse of (3).

OMOTE-NO-9: JODAN-AGE-UKE-CHUDANTSUKI (*Outside No. 9, Upper Step-Lift-Defence—Middle Step-Thrust*)

(1) You withdraw your right foot a pace to the rear and take up the left fudotachi posture. Thus your right fist is held at your right hip and your left fist raised above your forehead with the back of the fist turned inwards and the little finger uppermost as you sweep the fist upwards (Fig. 82). The opponent is supposed to defend himself against an upper body blow with a springing-up action (of the hands). According to the principle of defence you do not defend yourself with the wrist and back forearm alone. When your arm is swept up you lower your hips and defend yourself with your entire body. The reason for this is that if you defend yourself with only

your wrist and are confronting an opponent as strong as or stronger than yourself, you may fail to complete your defence. At the time of the defence the distance between the back of your fist and your forehead is about five or six inches. Your elbows are raised as much as possible to protect your own sides. Your upper body is slightly tilted forward.

(2) Your feet are in the same position. Your left fist is at your left hip and with your right fist you strike at the middle

Fig. 82

body of your imaginary opponent and at the same time utter the kiai shout.

(3) You bring back your right foot to its former position, lower both fists and resume the preparatory posture.

(4) The reverse movement of (1).

(5) The reverse movement of (2).

(6) The reverse movement of (3).

OMOTE-NO-10: JODAN-UCHIKOMI-CHUDANTSUKI *(Outside No. 10, Upper Step-Strike-in—Middle Step-Thrust)*

(1) You withdraw your right foot a pace to the rear and assume the left fudotachi posture with your right fist at your right hip and your left fist raised, the little finger edge upwards, as shown in Fig. 83, in front of your eyes and then to some degree in an oblique direction you deliver a downright blow. The distance of your left fist in front of your eyes is about one foot four inches as you look down upon it. The imaginary opponent may resist with the kentsui (hammer fist), the hand dealing the blow at his upper body or with his

69

wrist strike it down. On the other hand with the kentsui you may strike his face, &c.

(2)  Your feet in the same position, with your left fist at your left hip you strike with your right fist at your imaginary opponent's middle body. At the moment of the blow you utter the kiai shout.

Fig. 83

(3)  You bring back your feet to their former position, lower both fists and resume the preparatory posture.

(4)  The reverse of (1).

(5)  The reverse of (2).

(6)  The reverse of (3).

This movement completes the kata. You bring your left foot in line with your right foot to the heisokutachi posture and as at the beginning of the demonstration salute the Master who is superintending it ( see Fig. 71).

## TAIKYOKU KATA *(Essential Kata)*

### SHODAN *(First Step)*

The demonstration line (engisen) of the following three kata, see Taikyoku Shodan (First Step), Nidan (Second Step) and Sandan (Third Step) is in the shape of the Japanese character **I**. The demonstration line is the line drawn by the karateka when he practises these kata.  The white colored footmarks indicate the original position of the feet and the black  colored footmarks  their position after the relevant movement has been made. The line indicates the movement

70

of the feet. Following the Japanese author's example I have
considered it sufficient to indicate the movement lines, rang-
ing from a maximum of three to a minimum of two, under
the first figure only of the respective series; viz. Fig. 84, Fig.
120, Fig. 124, and Fig. 131. This arrangement seems clear
enough for all practical purposes.

As in every karate kata, before you begin to demonstrate
the Taikyoku Kata you salute standing, as shown in Fig. 84.

Fig. 84

| RIGHT | LEFT |
|-------|------|
| No.1 LINE | No.1 LINE |

←No.2 LINE

| RIGHT | LEFT |
|-------|------|
| No.3 LINE | No.3 LINE |

Fig. 85

*Preparation:* After the salutation you close your hands and
assume a posture in which you stand with both of them held
at your hips and your feet separated by a space of about one
foot five inches between them (Fig. 85). This is the outer
hachijitachi posture.

(Begin!)

(1) Your face is turned to the left and your left foot
advanced a pace to the left on No. 1 line. Your left hand, palm
opened and turned upwards, is held obliquely downwards
to the left. With a sort of reciprocal stretching movement and
as counter-action is applied, you close your palms and as
depicted in Fig. 86 with your left fist deliver a sweeping lower
body (gedanbarai) blow and place your right fist against your
right hip. At this stage you are in the left zenkutsutachi
posture. You are supposed to be defending yourself against

71

your opponent's attempt to strike or kick your sides. Your
left fist is held about six or seven inches above your left knee-
cap, the back of the fist turned upwards. Moreover both feet
are jointly drawn inwards.

(2)    Again your right foot is advanced a pace on the left
No. 1 line and you assume the right zenkutsutachi posture
with your left fist at your left hip (Fig. 87) and with your right
fist deliver a middle body blow (chudantsuki) at an imaginary

Fig. 86

Fig. 87

opponent. With your left hand you are supposed to grasp
your opponent's hand or leg and pull it towards you while
with your right fist you aim a blow at his chest.

(3)    Returning your right foot to the right No. 1 line you
keep your left foot as it is so that only the direction of the body
is changed. Your right hand is held from in front of your left
shoulder and your left hand directed right obliquely downwards. Reciprocally they describe a stretching movement and
as the force of reaction is applied you assume the right
zenkutsutachi posture, as shown in Fig. 88, and with your
right fist deal a sweeping lower body blow (gedanbarai) while
your left fist is brought to your left hip, i.e. a posture the exact
reverse in shape of (1).

(4)    With your left foot you take a pace on No. 1 line and
assume the left zenkutsutachi posture with your right fist held

72

Fig. 88

Fig. 89

Fig. 90

Fig. 91

at your right hip and at the same time, as shown in Fig. 89, with your left fist you deliver a frontal middle body blow (chudantsuki). Thus the movement is the exact opposite in shape to (2).

(5) With your right leg serving as axis you advance your left foot a pace on No. 2 line and, as shown in Fig. 90, assume the left zenkutsutachi posture and deliver a sweeping lower body blow (gedanbaraitsuki). This is a defence against a supposed attack from the front. Of course when your right fist is at your right hip the sweeping lower body blow is dealt with your left fist.

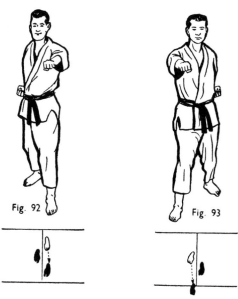

Fig. 92                    Fig. 93

(6) You take a pace forward with your right foot on No. 2 line and assume the right zenkutsutachi posture. Your left fist is at your left hip and, as shown in Fig. 91, with your right fist you deliver a middle body blow (chudantsuki).

(7) With your left foot you again take a pace forward and assume the left zenkutsutachi posture and as you hold your right fist at your right hip, (8) with your left fist you deliver a middle body blow (chudantsuki) (Fig. 92).

At the instant of the blow with your right fist you utter the kiai shout. Further, when as in (6), (7) and (8) the same kata is thrice repeated the blow for (7) is dealt with less

74

strength than for (6). Most strength is imparted to the (8) blow.

(9)   With your right leg serving as axis you advance your left foot a pace on the right No. 3 line and assume the left zenkutsutachi posture, your right fist at your right hip (Fig. 94), from which position with your left fist you deliver a sweeping lower body blow (gedanbaraitsuki).

(10)   Advancing your right foot on the right No. 3 line you

Fig. 94                    Fig. 95

assume the right zenkutsutachi posture with your left fist at your left hip and, as shown in Fig. 95, with your right fist deliver a middle body blow (chudantsuki).

(11)   Your left foot in the same position. You return your right foot leftward on No. 3 line and assume the right zenkutsutachi posture. As shown in Fig. 96, with your right fist you deliver a sweeping lower body blow (gedanbaraitsuki). Of course when your left fist is at your left hip you are prepared for the next attack.

(12)   Again with your left foot you take a pace forward on No. 3 line and assume the left zenkutsutachi posture, your right fist at your right hip, and at the same time, as shown in Fig. 97, with your left fist you deal a middle body blow (chudantsuki).

75

Fig. 96　　　　　　　　Fig. 97

(13)  With your right foot serving as axis you step forward a pace with your left foot on No. 2 line, i.e. you return to the original spot, and assume the left zenkutsutachi posture, and with your left fist deliver a sweeping lower body blow (gedanbaraitsuki), your right fist at your right hip (Fig. 98).

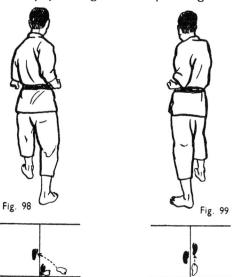

Fig. 98　　　　　　　　Fig. 99

(14) On No. 2 line you advance your right foot a pace forward and assume the right zenkutsutachi posture, your left fist at your left hip and, as shown in Fig. 99, with your right fist you deliver a middle body blow (chudantsuki).

(15) Again you advance your left foot a pace and assume the left zenkutsutachi posture with your right fist at your right hip, and simultaneously with your left fist, as shown in Fig. 100, deliver a middle body blow (chudantsuki).

(16) Once again you advance your right foot a pace and assume the right zenkutsutachi posture, your left fist at your

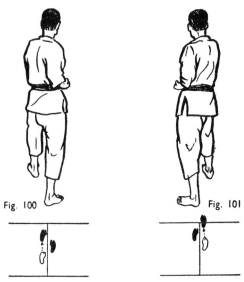

Fig. 100     Fig. 101

left hip and, as shown in Fig. 101, with your right fist deal a middle body blow (chudantsuki). At the instant of the right fist blow you utter the kiai shout.

(17) With your right leg serving as axis you advance your left foot on the left No. 1 line, assume the left zenkutsutachi posture and, as shown in Fig. 102, with your left fist deliver a sweeping lower body blow (gedanbaraitsuki).

(18) On No. 1 line you advance your right foot a pace leftward and simultaneously assume the right zenkutsutachi posture, your left fist at your left hip and, as shown in Fig. 103, with your right fist deal a middle body blow (chudantsuki), exactly the same as in the case of (2).

(19) You return your right foot to the right No. 1 line

77

Fig. 102

Fig. 103

and assume the right zenkutsutachi posture; then, as shown in Fig. 104, with your right fist you deliver a sweeping lower body blow (gedanbaraitsuki), your left fist at your left hip. The same as (3).

(20) On No. 1 line you advance your left foot a pace to

Fig. 104

Fig. 105

the right and assume the left zenkutsutachi posture with your right fist at your right hip and, as shown in Fig. 105, with your left fist deliver a middle body blow (chudantsuki). Exactly the same as (4).

(Halt!) Your right foot stays as it is and your left foot returns to the left to No. 1 line; both your fists are held in front of the thighs (Fig. 106). The closing action should be executed slowly. The opening and concluding positions of the demonstration must be the same.

*Salutation:* Both your legs are placed in regular order as you assume the heisokutachi or blocked foot posture and salute as at the commencement of the demonstration.

The so-called Pinan Kata which follows (from Shodan to

Fig. 106          Fig. 107          Fig. 108

Godan, i.e. First Step to Fifth Step) is the fundamental form of the so-called Shojukan-Ryu or school which originated from the Itosuha, an old karate school. The Taikyoku Kata, above described, is a simplified form of the Pinan Kata, and was devised by the celebrated karate Master Funakoshi for the purpose of making training easier.

PINAN SHODAN *(Pinan First Step)*

There are twenty-one movements in this step and like the

79

Taikyoku Kata the demonstration line is in the shape of the Japanese character ⊥.

(1) The same action as for the Taikyoku (1).

(2) The same action as for the Taikyoku (2).

(3) The same action as for the Taikyoku (3).

(4) Your left fist and left foot are simultaneously withdrawn. The space between your feet is roughly about equivalent to a little more than the width of your shoulders. Both knees are stretched. With your right fist from in front of your left shoulder you describe a large arc. You stop with your shoulders in a level position, as shown in Fig. 107. Your left fist is held at your left hip. If when from the zenkutsutachi posture you deal a sweeping lower body blow and the supposed opponent seizes your right wrist and shakes himself loose, you may retort with a kentsui (hammer fist) and beat down his wrist.

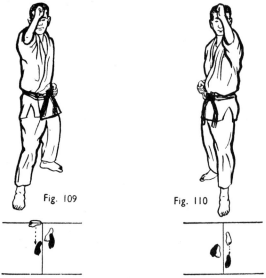

Fig. 109    Fig. 110

(5) The same as for the Taikyoku (4).

(6) The same as for the Taikyoku (5).

(7) Your right fist as it is. Your left fist is opened and your arm bent at the left elbow (Fig. 108) with the hand raised above your forehead. The back of your left hand is turned towards your forehead with about six or seven inches between them. If your contemplated lower body blow attack is warded

off by your supposed opponent and if he instantly retorts with a left fist blow at your face, you are supposed to defend yourself with your left wrist.

(8)  Your left leg as it is. Your right foot is advanced a pace on No. 2 line and both your knees are stretched. At the same time your left hand is withdrawn closed to your (left) hip. From down obliquely upwards your right arm is raised in front of your forehead and you assume the posture shown in Fig. 109. As you defend yourself with your left wrist against your opponent's left fist you are supposed to grasp his wrist and then twisting it in the reverse direction (gyaku) drive your right wrist against his left elbow. Moreover you are supposed to defend yourself against your opponent's upper body (jodan) attack. When you are accustomed to (7) and (8) you can execute them as a single movement.

(9)  Your right foot as it is. Your left foot is advanced a pace on No. 2 line. Your right fist is withdrawn to your right hip. Your left arm is held from down obliquely upwards and stretched in front of your forehead, as shown in Fig. 110. Opposite action to (8).

(10)  Your left foot as it is. Again you advance your right foot a pace on No. 2 line. Then with your right arm you execute an upper body-lift-defence (jodan-age-uke) and hold your left fist at your left hip. Precisely the same action as for (8).

(11) to (18) the action is wholly identical with the Taikyoku Shodan from (9) to (16). (17) and (18) are not described.

(19)  The sole of your right foot serving as axis, advance your left foot a pace on the left No. 1 line and assume the right kokutsutachi posture. Your right and left hands are opened, the back of your left hand outwards from the front of your right shoulder. Your right hand from the left obliquely applies reaction or recoil and you execute a middle body left tegatana defence as with your right hand forming a tegatana to attack the region of an imaginary opponent's solar-plexus, the back held horizontally, you assume the posture shown in Fig. 111. The middle body (literally "middle step") left tegatana defence posture is as follows: Your left elbow is slightly bent and the space between the elbow and side is about five or six inches. The height of the tegatana is about that of the shoulders. Your upper body is held with only your

face turned to the left. Among the Pinan Shodan this kata is regarded as the most difficult and you are urged to practise it seriously.

(20) With the sole of your left foot serving as axis you advance your right foot a pace to the left No. 1 line obliquely to the front and assume the left kokutsutachi posture. In contradistinction to (19) you adopt a right tegatana middle body defence as though to protect the chest. In order to defend the chest area the left tegatana held horizontally should be held near to the solar-plexus. Your face is turned looking

Fig. 111     Fig. 112

across your right shoulder at an imaginary opponent (Fig. 112).

(21) With the sole of your left foot serving as axis you return your right foot to No. 1 line and assume the left kokotsutachi posture. A right tegatana is held in front of your right shoulder and a left tegatana near to the solar-plexus with the back held horizontally downwards and your face turned to the right (Fig. 113).

(22) With the sole of your right foot serving as axis you advance your left foot obliquely to the front of the right No. 1 line and assume the right kokotsutachi posture. Your left hand is held as a left tegatana in front of your left shoulder and your right hand as a right tegatana near to the solar-

82

plexus with the back turned downwards horizontally, and your face is turned in the direction for a middle body left tegatana defence (Fig. 114).

(Halt!) Your right foot remains as it is, and your left foot is slowly returned to No. 1 line, both hands are closed and held in front of both thighs. You are now standing in the preparatory outer hachijitachi posture.

*Salutation:* After the demonstration you give the standing salutation in the previously described manner.

Fig. 113          Fig. 114

The foregoing explanation relates to twenty-two movements but actually since (7) and (8) become a single movement there are in all twenty-one movements.

PINAN NIDAN *(Second Step)*

There are in all twenty-six movements and the demonstration line is in the shape of the character. **I**.

(1) From the preparatory posture your right foot is stationary. Your left foot is advanced a pace on the left No. 1 line and you assume the right kokutsutachi posture. Simultaneously your left fist is raised in front of your left shoulder with the elbow bent and the back of the fist turned backwards. Your right fist is raised above your head, the back detached one or two inches from the forehead in the posture shown in Fig. 115. You ward off with your left wrist a

83

supposed opponent's attack against your face. With your right fist held above your head and your posture shifted to meet the next attack, your upper body is turned to the front and only your face is directed to the left.

(2) Both feet remain as they were. The back of your left fist is held downwards in front of your right shoulder. Simultaneously your upper body is twisted towards the left while your right fist describes a semi-circle and as it is held with the back downwards you strike in to the side (Fig. 116). With your left hand you seize your supposed opponent's

Fig. 115

Fig. 116

wrist and as you pull it towards you you deal a right kentsui (hammer fist) sideways.

(3) Both your feet remain as they are. The back of your left fist is turned upwards and as you thrust it forward horizontally to the left your right fist is brought to your right hip (Fig. 117). You strike in sideways with a right kentsui (hammer fist) and immediately with your left fist also deal a blow. Your upper body is turned to the front and your face to the left side.

(4) The position of both feet is as they were. Your left leg is stretched and you assume the left kokutsutachi posture and turn towards the right No. 1 line, the opposite to (1).

(5) The position of both feet as it is. The back of your

84

right fist is held downwards and drawn to the front of your right shoulder. Simultaneously with your left fist you describe a semi-circle and with the back turned downwards strike in sideways. The action is the reverse of (2).

(6)   Both your feet as they are. You extend your right fist horizontally and as you strike you bring your left fist to your left hip. The action is the reverse of (3).

(7)   Your left foot is brought back to its original position, i.e. the position at the time of the preparatory posture, and

Fig. 117                                        Fig. 118

is turned backwards and, as shown in Fig. 118, the sole of your right foot is raised to the front of your left knee-cap. The back of your right fist turned outwards is placed on top of your left fist which is held at your left hip.

(8)   Standing on your left leg with your right back fist you deal a blow at your supposed opponent's face and at the same time with a right ashigatana (footsword) kick his scrotum. The moment the attack is delivered your hand or foot must be withdrawn. As regards this action the purport is that when at the time of (6) posture you detect an attack from the rear you turn towards the back and simultaneously with hand or foot attack your opponent. Moreover as regards (7) and (8), when you become proficient you execute them as a single movement.

(9)   As you lower to the rear of No. 1 line the right foot with which you have dealt an upper kick you assume the right kokutsutachi posture and turning to the front, i.e. the top of No. 2 line, you assume a middle body left tegatana defence and a right tegatana near to your solar-plexus, horizontally, with the back held downwards. Refer for comparison to Pinan Shodan (19) Fig. 111.

(10)   On No. 2 line as you step forward a pace with your right foot you assume the left kokutsutachi posture and with your left hand defend yourself with a middle body tegatana. Refer for comparison to Pinan Shodan Fig. 110 and Fig. 111.

(11)   As you advance your left foot on No. 2 line you assume the right kokutsutachi posture and use your left hand as a middle body tegatana defence. Action the same as for (9).

(12)   Again you advance your right foot a pace on No. 2 line. This time both your knees are stretched. Then with a right four-finger nukite (the lengthwise nukite) you deal a middle body blow (chudantsuki) and at the same time draw a left tegatana to your right armpit. At this time the back of your hand seems to slide under your right armpit. The moment the blow is struck you utter the kiai shout. As regards this action, with your own hand you force down your supposed opponent's thrusting wrist and as you do so with a lengthwise four-finger nukite attack his solar-plexus.

(13)   The same as for the Pinan Shodan (19).

(14)   The same as for the Pinan Shodan (20).

(15)   The same as for the Pinan Shodan (21).

(16)   The same as for the Pinan Shodan (22).

(17)   Your right foot as it is. You advance your left foot a pace on No. 2 line and assume the left zenkutsutachi posture. At the same time with your left hand clenched and held with the back underneath at your left hip, with your right fist, back underneath, you take up the middle body inner defence (chudan-uchi-uke) (Fig. 119). With your right fist from the right obliquely downwards you describe a large semi-circle in front of your left shoulder as you take up the defence. Your right shoulder is brought forward and your left shoulder drawn back.

(18)   Your left foot and both fists as they are. With your right foot raised as high as possible you kick up to the front

of your right fist. With your right hand you grasp your supposed opponent's left wrist and kick against his twisted elbow joint in order to fracture it.

(19)   Your right foot which has given the kick is brought down on No. 2 line and at the same time, as the back of your right fist underneath is brought to your right hip, with the left fist you deal a middle body blow (chudantsuki).

(20)   Both feet as they are. Then the left fist which has dealt the middle body blow describes a semi-circle to the front of your right shoulder and as it turns you take up the middle body inner defence (chudan-uchi-uke). The posture is the reverse of (17).

Fig. 119

(21)   The action is the reverse of (18).

(22)   The action is the reverse of (19).

(23)   Your left foot as it is. Your right foot on No. 2 line steps out widely and you assume the right zenkutsutachi posture. Then as with your right wrist you adopt the middle body defence, back of fist underneath, your left fist is brought lightly in contact with your right elbow. This defensive method is called the both-hands defence, or morote-uke.

(24)   The same as the Pinan Shodan (1).

(25)   Your left foot as it is. Your left fist is opened and raised above your forehead. Simultaneously your right foot

87

is advanced right to the front, i.e. left obliquely to the front of the left No. 1 line. Both your knees are stretched. At the same time with your right fist you assume the upper body defensive position (jodan-uke) and bring your left fist to your left hip. The action of your hand is the same as for the Pinan Shodan (7) and (8).

(26) The same as for the Pinan Shodan (3).

(27) Exactly the same action as for (25). At the instant of the left fist upper body defence you utter the kiai shout.

(Halt!) You slowly return to the preparatory posture. Twenty-seven movements have been explained but since (7) and (8) are treated as a single movement there are in all twenty-six movements.

Fig. 120

RIGHT   LEFT   No.1
No.1 LINE   LINE

No.2 LINE

PINAN SANDAN *(Third Step)*

There are in all twenty-six movements. The demonstration line is in the shape of the character **T**.

(1) From the preparatory posture your right foot stays as it is while your left foot advances a pace on No. 1 line and at the same time you assume the right kokutsutachi posture. At the start your left fist is held in front of your left shoulder and your right fist is held from below. You stretch them reciprocally and complete the movement of defence as shown in Fig. 120. It is assumed that you are defending yourself

88

from an opponent's fist dealing a blow from the left side at your side. The height of the fist at the time of the defence is about the height of your shoulders. Your upper body is turned to the front while your face is pointed to the left.

(2) Your left foot stays as it is. Your right foot is drawn up to your left foot and points to the left and you stand in the heisokutachi or blocked foot posture. At the same time your right fist from outside your left elbow upwards and your left fist from the front of your right shoulder downwards reciprocally stretch, as shown in Fig. 121, and with your right

Fig. 121

fist you execute the middle body defence (chudan-uke), back of fist outside, and with your left fist the lower body defence (gedan-uke). At the moment when with your left hand you have warded off your imaginary opponent's right fist, he may suddenly withdraw his right fist and with his left fist and left foot together attack you. This changed defence is designed to cope with such a contingency with both your hands, i.e. your right fist for the middle body defence (chudan-uke) and your left fist for the lower body defence (gedan-uke). At the time your right arm is half bent and the distance between your elbow and chest is about five or six inches. The height at which your right fist is held is generally about the shoulder level. The gap betweens both your fists is about the width of your shoulders.

(3) Both your feet as they are in the heisokutachi posture. Your right fist from the inner side of your left elbow downwards and your left fist from the outside of your right elbow upwards are reciprocally stretched and with your right hand you get ready for a lower body defence (gedan-uke) and with your left hand for a middle body defence (chudan-uke). Your imaginary opponent again withdraws his left fist and left foot. This time when the attack is made with his right fist and right foot, with your left hand you make the middle body defence and with your right hand beat down his foot.

(4) Your left foot stays as it was. Your right foot is advanced on the right No. 1 line and simultaneously you assume the left kokutsutachi posture. With your right fist you adopt the middle body right side defence (chudan-migi-yoko-uke), your left fist held at your left hip. This action is the reverse of (1).

(5) Your right foot as it was. Your left foot is drawn up to your right foot and points to the right and you assume the heisokutachi posture. At the same time with your left hand your assume the middle body defence (chudan-uke) and with your right hand the lower body defence (gedan-uke). The action is the reverse of (2).

(6) In the same posture. Your right hand is held in the middle body defence and your left hand in the lower body defence. The action is the reverse of (3).

(7) Your right foot as it was. Your left foot is advanced a pace on No. 2 line and at the same time you assume the right kokutsutachi posture. Your left hand is held in a left tegatana defence and your right hand in a right tegatana defence at the level of your solar-plexus. The posture is the same as for the Pinan Shodan (19).

(8) Your left foot as it was. Your right foot advances a pace on No. 2 line and at the same time your left tegatana with the back above is at your right armpit and your right hand in a four-finger lengthwise nukite deals a frontal middle body thrust. With your left hand you are supposed to check your opponent's middle body attacking right wrist, draw it towards you and from over (his) left wrist thrust a four-finger lengthwise nukite at his solar-plexus.

90

(9)   As shown in Fig. 122 you bring back the four-finger lengthwise nukite inversely (a left turn) and with your right foot as axis make a single revolution. Your left foot on No. 2 line advances a pace and you assume the kibatachi (equestrian) posture. Simultaneously the back of a left kentsui (hammer fist) held upwards, stretched horizontally to the shoulders, deals a lateral blow. Your right fist is held at your

Fig. 122

right hip and your face points to the front. If your opponent deflects your nukite and twists your wrist in the reverse direction you twist your body and as you do so turn your right hand inversely to the back and make a revolution to the left. Then with a left kentsui you are supposed to strike his side.

(10)   Your left foot as it was. Your right foot advances a pace on No. 2 line and at the same time you assume the right zenkutsutachi posture. With your right fist you deal a middle body blow and bring your left fist to your left hip. As the blow is dealt you utter the kiai shout.

(11)   Your right foot as it was. Your left foot is drawn up to your right foot and as you make a left turn and face the rear you assume the heisokutachi posture. At the same time the backs of both your fists are directed forward and held at both

hips. Your shoulders are lowered and both elbows stretched. These movements should be executed slowly.

(12) Your left foot as it was. Your right foot lifted high with the knee bent on No. 2 line takes a step to the rear. Your right fist is at your right hip and you draw back your right elbow and apply counteraction. Your right foot touches the ground and at the same time you assume the kibatachi posture. Your right elbow makes the defence. At this time of course it is at your hip. With your right foot you are supposed to trample crushingly on your opponent's shin and at the same time with your right elbow strike his solar-plexus or ward off your opponent's attack and swing your right elbow to the front. Your face is pointed to the front, i.e. to the back of No. 2 line.

(13) The same position. In that upright posture you deal with your right back fist from the front of your right shoulder a downright blow to the lateral right rear of No. 2 line. With the back of the fist you are supposed to strike the jinchu (spot under the nose called the philtrum) of an opponent standing on the right side. Your elbow is slightly bent and your fist, the back underneath, is held at shoulder height.

(14) In the same upright posture, the back of your right fist turned to the front and brought back to your right hip. (13) and (14) are executed swiftly and without a break.

(15) Your right foot as it was. So as not to cause the posture of your upper body to be broken, with your left foot you step to the rear on No. 2 line and at the same time assume the kibatachi (equestrian) posture and use a left empi. The reverse of (12).

(16) In the same posture with your left back fist, starting from the front of your left shoulder to the left side and the back pointing downwards, you deal a downright blow. The movement is the reverse of (13).

(17) In the same posture you take to the left hip your left fist with its back to the front. The movement is the reverse of (14). (16) and (17) are executed swiftly and without a break.

(18) The same movement as (12).

(19) The same movement as (13).

(20) The same movement as (14). From (12) to (20) the same movements are repeated three times but the second time the action is lightly executed and the third time the maximum strength is imparted to the action.

(21) Your right foot as it was. Your left foot is again advanced a pace to the rear of No. 2 line. At the same time turning to the front you assume the left zenkutsutachi posture. Your right fist is at your right hip with the back underneath and with your left fist you deal a middle body blow (chudan-tsuki).

(22) Your left foot as it was. Your right foot is advanced to the right front on No. 1 line in line with your left foot. Then your right foot serving as axis is turned to the left on the left No. 1 line and your left foot advances a big pace as you assume the kibatachi posture. At the same time with your right elbow bent your right fist is swung over your left shoulder with the back uppermost for an upper thrust. Your left fist is sufficiently drawn to the rear and your face points

Fig. 123

to the front (Fig. 123). Assuming that an opponent attempts to embrace you from behind you lower your hips and adopt the kibatachi posture and with your right fist deal a blow at his face and with your left elbow a blow at the side of his chest.

(23) In the kibatachi posture as your feet approach the right, the opposite to (22), your left fist is thrust up over your right shoulder and your right elbow drawn sufficiently to the rear.

93

(Halt!) Your left foot as it was. Your right foot is brought to the left as you revert to the preparatory posture.

Since (13), (14), (16), (17), (19) and (20) are executed as a single movement, on the basis of their similarity, twenty movements in all are credited to this division.

PINAN YODAN *(Fourth Step)*

There are twenty movements. The demonstration line is practically in the shape of the character **I**.

(1) From the preparatory posture your right foot as it was. Your left foot is advanced on No. 1 line to the left and you assume the right kokutsutachi posture. At the same time both your hands are opened as tegatana according to the principle of Fig. 115. The right tegatana, elbow bent and the back turned inside, is raised above your forehead. The left tegatana, elbow bent and the back turned to the rear side, is raised and

Fig. 124

| RIGHT | LEFT |
|-------|------|
| No.1 LINE | No.1 LINE |

←No.2 LINE

| RIGHT | LEFT |
|-------|------|
| No.3 LINE | No.3 LINE |

turned inwards. In the style of the Pinan Nidan (1) both fists are in the opened shape. Your upper body is straight and your shoulders are not stretched. According to this kata with your left hand you ward off your opponent's wrist, seize that wrist and as you pull it towards you, with your right tegatana you strike his carotid artery, jinchu, &c.

(2) Both feet as they were. You assume the left koku-

94

tsutachi posture with your face turned to the right. A left tegatana with the back turned inwards is raised above your forehead. A right tegatana with the back turned to the rear is held in front of your right shoulder with the elbow bent. The posture is the opposite to (1).

(3) Your right foot as it was. Your left foot takes a large step on No. 2 line and simultaneously you assume the left zenkutsutachi posture. Both your fists are crossed. The backs of both hands are joined in front with the right wrist on top, as shown in Fig. 124, and in a lower body stance (gedan) you thrust them out. Both your fists are separated from your body about six or seven inches. Both elbows are sufficiently stretched. Your upper body is held upright and your eyes gaze to the front. When an imaginary opponent tries to kick your scrotum you are supposed to fend his shin off with both fists.

(4) Your left foot as it was. Your right foot takes a big step forward on No. 2 line and you assume the left kokutsutachi posture. With your right arm you make a middle body defence (chudan-uke), the back of your hand turned downwards and the height of the fist about that of the shoulders. Your left fist is held with its back downwards and held lightly in contact with your right elbow. Of course the action of both your hands takes place simultaneously. This method of defence is called the Sasae-Uke, or Propping Defence.

(5) Your right foot as it was. Your left foot is drawn up to your right foot and your face is turned to the left. Your right fist is at your right hip with the back held downwards. Your left fist, the back in front, is placed lightly on top of it. The sole of your left foot is raised above your right knee and slightly separated from it. The posture is the reverse of Fig. 118.

(6) You stand on your right leg, as shown in Fig. 125, and as with your left back fist pointing to the left you deal a blow at your imaginary opponent's face, with a left ashigatana (footsword) you attack him in another part of his body, not here specified but doubtless in the area of the midriff or lower still, the scrotum. When you are sufficiently skilled (5) and (6) are executed as a single movement.

(7) With your left foot you step down on the left No. 3 line and assume the left zenkutsutachi posture. Simultaneously twisting your upper body to the left, as shown in

Fig. 126, you assume the posture for an empi attack. With your left palm you strike the outside of your right elbow. When against an opponent on the left you attack his face with the back of your left fist and with a left ashigatana kick his side or scrotum and with a right empi strike his chest when the back of the fist points outwards and the distance from the opponent's chest is about five or six inches. In this right empi the significance of the left palm attack is as follows: Grasping your opponent's hand and pulling it towards you you are supposed to use the empi to attack his chest, extend the left hand and deal him a blow with your right elbow. Thus two methods are employed.

(8) Your left foot as it was. Your right foot is brought up

Fig. 125          Fig. 126

to your left foot and your face is turned to the right while your left fist with the back downwards is taken to your left hip and your right fist with the back in front is placed on it. The sole of your right foot is raised above your left knee. The position is the same as in Fig. 118.

(9) You stand on your left foot. Turning to the right you strike with your right back fist and kick with a right ashigatana. (8) and (9) are executed as a single movement.

(10) With your right foot you step forward on No. 3 line

96

and assume the right zenkutsutachi posture. Simultaneously you twist your upper body to the right and thrusting with a left empi, with your right palm strike the outside of your left elbow. The opposite action to (6).

(11) The position of both your feet is the same. Both your knees are stretched and your body is turned to the front. At the same time your right hand is opened and the back brought in contact with your forehead. From the front of your forehead you describe a large semi-circle to the right. The back of your hand is held downwards and as it strikes to the front with a left tegatana you execute an upper body defence (jodan-uke), the back of the hand in contact with your forehead. It is supposed that if your opponent attacks from the front you strike his wrist with a left tegatana.

(12) In the same posture, as shown in Fig. 127, you lift

Fig. 127          Fig. 128

your right foot as high as possible and kick forward with it.

(13) As you kick you step smartly forward a pace with your right foot and resting on that foot and keeping pace with it you draw your left lightly behind it. Your right hand once extended to the front, after being withdrawn to the front of your chest, used as a back fist, deals a frontal upper body blow (jodantsuki). Your left hand held above your forehead

97

it now stretched to the front and brought to your left hip (Fig. 128). When you strike to the front with your right back fist you utter the kiai shout. Your left hand is clenched fist-like, the back downwards, and brought to your left hip. The actions (12) and (13) are executed as a single movement.

(14)   Your right foot serving as axis and as you swivel your body to the left you step a pace forward with your left foot obliquely on the right No. 3 line and assume the left zenkutsu-tachi posture. Simultaneously you cross both fists, the right fist uppermost and the backs of both fists turned outwards. In this position they exert pressure against each other as though thrusting each other aside to left and right. When you

Fig. 129

thrust both fists aside to left and right both elbows are slightly bent. The distance between both fists is about the width of the shoulders and the backs of the fists are turned outwards. You are supposed to ward off your opponent's two-hand thrust with your wrists which push aside his hands to left and right.

(15)   In the same position with your right foot you kick up high between both fists (Fig. 129).

(16)   You step down to the front with the foot which has been raised to kick and assume the right zenkutsutachi posture. Then as you bring your left fist to your left hip with

your right fist you deliver a middle body blow (chudantsuki).

(17)   Both your feet as they were. Your right fist at your right hip, with your left fist you deliver a middle body blow (chudantsuki). When (16) and (17) are executed continuously as consecutive movements they are called "renzokutsuki", or "continuous blow or thrust". (15), (16) and (17) are executed as a single movement.

(18)   Your left foot as it was. Your right foot is advanced a pace obliquely right between No. 2 and left No. 3 lines and you assume the right zenkutsutachi posture. Both your fists are crossed, the right fist on top, the backs of both fists turned outwards, and they push each other aside to left and right. The backs of both fists as before are turned outwards. The opposite foot position to (14).

(19)   In the same posture you kick up high between both fists.

(20)   As you step a pace forward with the left foot which has just kicked up you assume the left zenkutsutachi posture. Your right fist is brought to your right hip and with your left fist you deal a middle body blow (chudantsuki). When a middle body blow is dealt do not strike with the left fist once it has been withdrawn but strike immediately from the (19) posture without drawing back the left fist. This method is the same as (16).

(21)   In the same posture, as you withdraw your left fist to your left hip you deal a middle body blow (chudantsuki) with your right fist. (19), (20) and (21) are executed as a single movement.

(22)   Your right foot as it was. Your left foot advances a pace obliquely left, i.e. on No. 2 line, and you assume the right kokutsutachi posture. With your left fist you adopt the frontal middle body defence (back of hand turned downwards) and your right fist is held in contact with the under part of your left elbow. This method of defence is called the "morote chudan-uke", or "both hands middle body defence", and alternatively "sasae-uke", or "propping defence". Your body is turned to the right and your face to the front, to the rear of No. 2 line.

(23)   Your left foot as it was. Your right foot on No. 2 line takes a step to the rear and you assume the left zenkutsutachi posture. Simultaneously with your right fist you adopt a

99

frontal middle body defence and bring the little finger edge of your left fist into contact with the under part of your right elbow. Of course the action of both fists takes place together. It is the opposite action to (22).

(24) Both your hands are opened and their palms opposite to each other as soon as they are raised high above your head. As shown in Fig. 130, as you lift up your right knee you close both hands and draw them down left and right under that knee. With both hands you are supposed to grasp your opponent's head and as you drag it downwards drive your

Fig. 130

right knee-cap against his face. The instant you raise your right knee you utter the kiai shout.

(25) With your right foot you take a forward step and at the same time turning to the rear assume the right kokutsutachi posture. Both feet in that position make a left turn. A right tegatana with the palm uppermost is held horizontally near to your solar-plexus and with a left tegatana you adopt the middle body defence. The posture is the same as (19) Pinan Shodan.

(26) Your left foot as it was. Your right foot advances a step on No. 2 line and you assume the left kokutsutachi posture. The back of a left tegatana turned downwards is held

100

in front of your chest, and with a right tegatana you adopt a middle body defence. This is the opposite to (25).

(Halt!) Your left foot as it was. Your right foot is withdrawn as you assume the outer hachijitachi posture. Both the tegatana are lowered and you assume the preparatory posture. These actions are slowly performed.

PINAN GODAN (*Pinan 5th Step*)

There are in all twenty-two movements. The demonstration line is in the shape of the character T.

(1) The preparatory posture is the same as for the Pinan Sandan (1).

(2) You assume the right kokutsutachi posture. Your upper body is twisted to the left and with your right fist

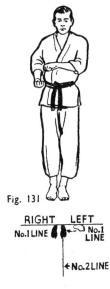

Fig. 131

RIGHT    LEFT
No.1 LINE              No.1 LINE
                       ← No.2 LINE

turned to the left you execute a middle body blow (chudan-tsuki) and at the same time bring your left fist to your left hip.

(3) Your left foot as it was. Your right foot is drawn up to your left foot and you assume the heisokutachi posture. Your face is turned to the right, your right fist is drawn to your right hip, and, as shown in Fig. 131, your left fist is held in front of your chest about five or six inches from your chest at the solar-plexus. This action combining face, hands and

101

feet is executed slowly. A sensation of slightly lowering the tip of the left fist is imparted and it is held in the direction of your right flank.

(4)  Action the same as for the Pinan Sandan (4).

(5)  Action left and right the opposite to (2).

(6)  Action left and right the opposite to (3).

(7)  The same as for the Pinan Yodan (22).

(8)  The same as for the Pinan Yodan (3). This method of defence is called the "Juji-uke", or "Figure - Ten Defence", and the "Kosa-uke" (Intersecting Defence).

(9)  Your lower body in the same posture. As shown in Fig. 132, with the juji-uke both your hands are raised above your head opened and crossed at the wrists. This action must be done swiftly. When guarding against a lower body attack

Fig. 132          Fig. 133

and your opponent successively makes an upper body attack, both your hands held in the lower body juji-uke are instantly raised to the upper body for defence.

(10)  Your lower body in the same posture. Both your wrists are joined with both palms opened opposite each other. At the same time your left wrist is pressed against the other and you adopt the posture shown in Fig. 133. At the moment when you have effected a jodan-juji-uke (upper body juji defence) and your opponent again strikes with his left fist

102

you are supposed to stop and ward off his attack. Both your crossed hands (the palm of the right hand turned upwards and the palm of the left hand downwards) are held about a foot in front of your chest.

(11)   The lower part of your body is in the same position. As with your left fist you deal a blow to the front you bring your right fist to your right hip.

(12)   Your left foot as it was. Your right foot is advanced a step on No. 2 line and you assume the right zenkutsutachi posture. At the same time with your right fist, you deal a middle body blow and bring your left fist to your left hip. At the instant you strike with your right fist you utter the kiai shout.

(13)   With your left foot serving as axis you switch to the left and transfer to the rear your right foot on No. 2 line and

Fig. 134

then adopt the kibatachi posture. At the same time with your right fist you deal a sweeping lower body blow (gedanbarai-tsuki). Your left fist is held at your left hip. Your face is turned in the direction of the lower body blow, i.e. the rear of No. 2 line.

(14)   Your lower body is in the same posture. Your face is turned in the opposite direction, i.e. the front of No. 2 line.

103

Simultaneously while your right fist is at your right hip your opened left hand is stretched to the left. With your left wrist you are supposed to be warding off a middle body blow proceeding from No. 2 front line (the left direction). Fig. 134 shows the posture of the upper half of your body.

(15). Your left foot as it was. As shown in Fig. 134 with your right foot you kick your outstretched left palm. With your left hand you are supposed to grasp your opponent's right wrist and as you pull him towards yourself kick his chest. This method of kicking is known as the "mikkazuki-keri" or "three-day moon kick". When kicking in this style your left hand is not lowered and you must kick high.

(16) The right foot with which you have kicked is stepped down in the direction of the front of No. 2 line and as you assume the kibatachi posture, with a right empi

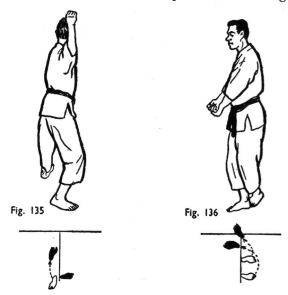

Fig. 135       Fig. 136

you strike against your left palm (which is representing an opponent). The back of your hand is turned outwards and the space between it and your chest is about five or six inches.

(17) Your right foot as it was. Your left foot is retracted to the rear of your right foot and lightly in contact with it. Your right knee is slightly bent and you stand on your right leg. Your face is turned to the right, i.e. towards the front of No.

104

2 line. At the same time with your right fist turned to the right and the back of the hand underneath you make a middle body defence and your left fist, back of hand underneath, is brought lightly against your right elbow.

(18) Your right leg is slightly bent and supports the weight of your body. Your face is turned to the rear (rear of No. 2 line) and, as shown in Fig. 135, your right fist is stretched upwards, your left fist at your right elbow (not shown in that figure). Simultaneously your left foot is stretched to the left with the tips of the toes lightly touching the ground. Your bust is slightly tilted to the right. From your right fist obliquely to the tip-toes of your left foot a straight line is formed.

(19) Your right foot is placed on the ground and you jump to the rear of No. 2 line as high as possible and the line drawn by this movement should be as wide as possible. As shown in Fig. 136, your right knee is slightly bent and your left foot is brought behind your right foot and lightly against it. Both your fists are crossed, the backs of both upwards and the right

Fig. 137

fist on top in which posture you make a lower body defence (gedan-uke). Your face is turned to the front, i.e. to the right of No. 2 line.

(20) Your left foot is stretched and with your right foot you take a wide step to the right to the rear of No. 2 line and

assume the right zenkutsutachi posture. At the same time with the back of your right fist underneath you take up a middle body defence against the right direction, i.e. the rear of No. 2 line. Your left fist, its back underneath, is lightly applied to your right elbow and your face is turned to the right.

(21) This time you are in the right kokutsutachi posture. Your face is turned to the rear (the front of No. 2 line). Your palm uppermost above your left knee, you strike with a right tegatana, and a left tegatana, the palm uppermost, is held in front of your right shoulder. At the same time your left and right hands are reciprocally tightened; while they are firmly clenched, with the right fist you adopt an upper body defence (jodan-uke). In this posture your right arm is raised behind your head, the back turned outwards. With your left fist you adopt a lower body defence (gedan-uke). Your left hand is parallel to your left leg (Fig. 137).

(22) Your bust and right foot as they were. Your left foot is drawn up to your right foot.

(23) Your left foot as it is. You make a left turn with your right foot, advance it to the right (the front of No. 2 line) and assume the left kokutsutachi posture. Simultaneously you strike in with a left tegatana above your right knee, the palm uppermost, and a right tegatana, the palm uppermost, in front of your left shoulder. Simultaneously both hands are reciprocally tightened. With your left fist you adopt an upper body defence (jodan-uke) and with your right fist a lower body defence (gedan-uke). This is the opposite to (6).

(Halt!) Your left foot as it is. Your right foot is drawn up to it and you assume the outer hachijitachi posture and then revert to the preparatory posture.

The explanation covers twenty-three movements but since actually (15) and (16) are executed as a single movement there are in all twenty-two movements.

Roundhouse Kick
to head.

Elbow Smash to face
and Wrist Grasp.

A Lunge Punch at the left is met with a Reverse Punch by opponent on right.

B

**Knifehand Strike to temple.**

C

**A Rising Block.**

D

**Grasping technique with Backfist Punch.**

**Elbow Smash to neck.**

E

Roundhouse Kick
to the temple.

Blocking a Straight
Punch and counter-
ing with a punch
to the ribs.

F

CHAPTER VIII

KATA OF KUMITE—YAKUSOKU KUMITE—TANSHIKI KUMITE—
FUKUSHIKI KUMITE—JIYU KUMITE

In the karate terminology, when kata or forms are being
demonstrated by two partners, in contradistinction to judo the
assailant is called Semete (not Tori) and the partner attacked
Ukete instead of Uke. And as already explained elsewhere
in these pages the karate name for contest is kumite. The first
type of kumite kata I shall try to describe is often called
yakusoku kata, literally "agreement kata", because it is
demonstrated in a strictly pre-arranged manner as in judo.

URA-NO-1: GEDANBARAI-CHUDANTSUKI *(Reverse* 1: *Lower
Step Sweep—Middle Step-Thrust)*

Before the demonstration of the kumite kata, as in that of

Fig. 138

all other kata, the performers salute the presiding Shihan or
Master, in the style described for the first Ten-no-Kata (see
Fig. 71). Semete and Ukete then face each other with a distance between them of about three feet in the outer hachijitachi posture (Fig. 138) and afterwards salute each other (Fig.
139).

107

At the word of command to prepare, Semete (on the left) withdraws his right foot a pace, assumes the left zenkutsu-tachi posture and poises his left fist for delivery of a sweeping lower body blow or gedanbaraitsuki. His right fist is at his right hip and he gazes straight at his opponent's eyes.

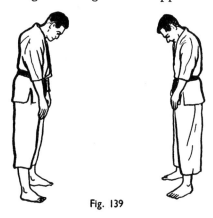

Fig. 139

Ukete stands in the outer hachijitachi posture and also gazes straight at his opponent's eyes. Whatever the nature of attack it is imperative that both performers should preserve an unmoved mental attitude in both defence and attack.

Fig. 140

(1) At the word of command Semete utters the kiai shout, steps forward a pace with his left foot and assumes the left zenkutsutachi posture, then with his right fist directs

a blow at Ukete's lower abdomen. Simultaneously he withdraws his left fist to his left hip.

Ukete withdraws his right foot a pace to the rear, assumes the left zenkutsutachi posture and with his left fist addressed

Fig. 141

for the gedanbaraitsuki or lower sweep sweeps away Semete's right wrist from inside and brings his right fist to his right hip (Fig. 141).

Fig. 142

(2)   At the word of command Semete assumes the posture for gedantsuki or lower body thrust and and fixes his gaze on his opponent.

Ukete brings his left fist to his left hip and uttering the

109

kiai shout aims a blow with his right fist at Semete's chest area (Fig. 142).

(3) At the word of command Semete withdraws his right foot to the preparatory posture, i.e. the outer hachijitachi.

Ukete advances his right foot to the preparatory posture.

At the preparatory word of command Semete retracts his left foot a pace to the rear and assumes the right zenkutsu-tachi posture, addresses his right fist for the sweeping lower body blow or gedanbaraitsuki, and places his left fist against his left hip.

Ukete also assumes the preparatory posture, in this case the exact opposite to Semete in Fig. 140 as regards the position of both hands and both feet.

(1) At the word of command Semete steps forward a pace with his left foot and assumes the left zenkutsutachi posture.

Fig. 143

Then uttering the kiai shout he aims a blow with his left fist at Ukete's lower body (gedan) and at the same time brings his right fist to his right hip.

Ukete withdraws his left foot and assumes the right zenkutsutachi posture and as he defends himself with his right fist in a sweeping lower body style he brings his left fist to his left hip (Fig. 143).

(2) At the word of command Semete assumes the same posture.

Ukete places his right fist against his hip, utters the kiai shout and with his left fist deals a middle body thrust (chudantsuki) at Semete (Fig. 144).

110

(3) At the word of command Semete withdraws his left foot to the preparatory posture.

Ukete advances his left foot to the preparatory posture.

When the foregoing movements are each executed twice,

Fig. 144

then after the first demonstration Semete and Ukete exchange roles and practise them again twice each. The same rule applies to the rest of the kata.

Fig. 145

URA-NO-2: CHUDAN-UDE-UKE—CHUDANTSUKI *(Reverse 2: Middle Step-Arm-Defence—Middle Step-Thrust)*

At the preparatory word of command Semete from the outer hachijitachi posture with his right foot takes a pace to the rear and assumes the left zenkutsutachi posture. His left fist

111

is poised for a sweeping lower body blow (gedantsuki) and his right fist is held at his right hip.

Ukete stands in the same preparatory posture.

(1) At the word of command Semete steps forward a pace with his right foot and assumes the right zenkutsutachi posture with his left fist at his left hip, utters the kiai shout and with his right fist delivers a middle body blow (chudantsuki).

UKETE withdraws his right foot a pace and assumes the left fudotachi posture with his right fist at his right hip and at the same time with his left fist (the thumb edge of the wrist) wards off Semete's attack with a sweeping blow to deflect his wrist outwards (Fig. 145).

(2) At the word of command Semete assumes the same posture.

Ukete with his left fist at his left hip utters the kiai shout and with his right fist aims a middle body blow (chudantsuki) at Semete (Fig. 146).

Fig. 146

(3) At the word of command Semete takes a pace to the rear with his right foot and assumes the preparatory posture.

Ukete advances a pace with his right foot and assumes the preparatory posture.

At the preparatory word of command Semete withdraws his left foot a pace to the rear and assumes the right zenkutsu-tachi posture and at the same time with his right fist poised for a sweeping lower body blow (gedanbaraitsuki) holds his left fist at his left hip.

112

Ukete is in the preparatory posture.

(1) At the word of command Semete steps forward a pace with his left foot and assumes the left zenkutsutachi posture with his right fist at his right hip. Then uttering the kiai shout and with his left fist he aims a middle body blow (chudantsuki) at Ukete.

Ukete withdraws his left foot a pace to the rear and assumes the right fudotachi posture, and with the wrist of his right fist sweeps Semete's attacking arm to the outside and places his left fist against his left hip (Fig. 147).

Fig. 147

(2) At the word of command Semete is in the same posture. Ukete, his right fist held at his right hip and as he utters the kiai shout, delivers a middle body blow (chudantsuki) with his left fist (Fig. 148).

(3) At the word of command Semete withdraws his left foot a pace and assumes the preparatory posture.

Ukete advances his left foot a pace and also assumes the preparatory posture. Afterwards Semete and Ukete exchange roles and repeat the practice.

URA-NO-3: CHUDAN-TEGATANA-UKE-CHUDAN-NUKITE (Reverse 3: Middle Step-Handsword-Defence—Middle Step-Piercing Hand)

At the preparatory word of command Semete from the preparatory posture (outer hachijitachi) withdraws his right foot a pace and assumes the left zenkutsutachi posture. His left fist is poised for delivery of a sweeping lower body blow (gedanbaraitsuki), and his right fist is at his right hip.

113

Ukete is in the preparatory posture.

(1) At the word of command Semete takes a step to the front with his right foot and assumes the right zenkutsutachi posture with his left fist at his left hip. At the same time he

Fig. 148

utters the kiai shout and with his right fist aims a middle body blow (chudantsuki) at Ukete.

Ukete withdraws his right foot a pace to the rear, assumes the right kokutsutachi posture and with a left tegatana

Fig. 149

directed from the inside outwards, slightly slantwise, sweeps aside his opponent's right wrist (Fig. 149).

(2) At the word of command Semete assumes the same posture.

Ukete relaxes his left tegatana, clenches his fingers and

114

brings the hand to his left hip. At the same time opening his right fist he delivers a nukite (piercing hand) to his opponent's middle body. He utters the kiai shout (Fig. 150).

(3) At the word of command Semete withdraws his right fist and assumes the preparatory posture.

Ukete advances his right foot and assumes the preparatory posture.

At the preparatory word of command Semete retracts his left foot a pace and assumes the right zenkutsutachi posture with his left fist at his left hip and his right fist poised to deliver a sweeping lower body blow (gedanbaraitsuki).

Fig. 150

Ukete is in the preparatory posture.

(1) At the word of command Semete advances his left foot a pace and assumes the left zenkutsutachi posture with his right fist at his right hip. Uttering the kiai shout and with his left fist he aims a middle body blow (chudantsuki) at his opponent.

Ukete withdraws his left foot a pace to the rear and assumes the left kokutsutachi posture with his left fist at his left hip. His right hand is opened in the tegatana shape and from the inside outwards and slightly obliquely he sweeps away his opponent's left wrist. This manoeuvre is known as a chudan-tegatana-uke or middle step-handsword-defence (Fig. 151).

(2) At the word of command Semete assumes the same posture.

Ukete with his right hand clenched at his right hip and his

115

left hand opened aims a nukite (piercing hand) at his opponent's middle body to the accompaniment of the kiai shout.

(3) At the word of command Semete retracts his left foot and assumes the preparatory posture.

Fig. 151

Ukete advances his left foot and also assumes the preparatory posture.

At the close of the foregoing movements Semete and Ukete exchange roles and repeat the practice.

Fig. 152

URA-NO-4: JODAN-TEGATANA-HARAI-JODANTSUKI *(Reverse 4: Upper Step-Handsword Sweep—Upper Step-Thrust)*

(1) At the preparatory word of command Semete with-

116

draws his right foot a pace and assumes the left zenkutsutachi posture. Concurrently he holds his right fist at his right hip and his left fist in the sweeping lower body position (gedan-barai).

Ukete stands in the preparatory posture.

Semete takes a big step forward with his right foot and assumes the right zenkutsutachi posture, with his left fist at his left hip. Then uttering the kiai shout he directs with his right fist an upper body blow (jodantsuki) at his opponent.

Ukete withdraws his right foot and assumes the left fudo-tachi posture with his right fist at his right hip and with a left-hand tegatana wards off his opponent's right-wrist attack (Fig. 153).

Fig. 153

(2) At the word of command Semete assumes the same posture.

With his left hand Ukete grasps his opponent's right wrist and with a twisting action draws it towards himself. Then to the accompaniment of the kiai shout he deals with his right fist a blow at his opponent's upper body (jodan) which includes the face (Fig. 154).

(3) At the word of command Semete withdraws his right foot to the preparatory posture.

Ukete advances his right foot, relinquishes his left-hand grip on Semete's right wrist and assumes the preparatory posture.

117

At the preparatory word of command Semete from the preparatory posture withdraws his left foot a pace to the rear and assumes the right zenkutsutachi posture with his left

Fig. 154

hand at his left hip and his right fist in the sweeping lower body blow position (gedanbaraitsuki).

Ukete stands in the preparatory posture.

(1)   At the word of command Semete advances a pace with

Fig. 155

his left foot and assumes the left zenkutsutachi posture with his right fist at his right hip. Then uttering the kiai shout and with his left fist he aims a blow at his opponent's face.

Ukete withdrawing his left foot a pace assumes the right

118

fudotachi posture with his left fist at his left hip and with a right tegatana to his opponent's left wrist wards off the blow (Fig. 155).

(2) At the word of command Semete assumes the same posture.

Ukete with his right hand grasps his opponent's left wrist and with a twisting sensation draws it towards himself; then to the accompaniment of the kiai shout and with his left fist deals a blow at his opponent's upper body (Fig. 156).

Fig. 156

(3) At the word of command Semete withdraws his left foot and assumes the preparatory posture.

Ukete withdraws his left foot, lets go his hold on his opponent's left wrist and assumes the preparatory posture.

As before Semete and Ukete then change roles and twice repeat the movement.

URA-NO-5: JODAN-AGE-UKE-CHUDANTSUKI (*Reverse* 5: *Upper Step-Lift Defence—Middle Step-Thrust*)

At the preparatory word of command Semete withdraws his right foot a pace and assumes the left zenkutsutachi posture, with his right fist at his right hip, and his left fist poised for delivery of a sweeping lower body blow (gedanbaraitsuki).

Ukete is in the preparatory posture.

(1) At the word of command Semete steps forward with his right foot and assumes the right zenkutsutachi posture,

119

his left fist at his left hip, and uttering the kiai shout and with his right fist aims a blow at Ukete's upper body.

Ukete draws back his right foot a pace and assumes the left fudotachi posture, his right fist at his right hip. Then with

Fig. 157

the wrist of his left fist he springs up his opponent's right hand and wards off the blow (Fig. 157).

(2) At the word of command Semete assumes the same posture.

Fig. 158

Ukete, his left fist at his left hip, utters the kiai shout and with his right fist deals a blow at Semete's middle body (chudan) (Fig. 158).

120

(3) At the word of command Semete withdraws his right foot to the preparatory posture.

Ukete advances his right foot and assumes the preparatory posture.

At the preparatory word of command Semete withdraws his left foot a pace and assumes the right zenkutsutachi posture, his left fist at his left hip and his right fist poised for a sweeping lower body blow (gedanbaraitsuki).

Ukete is in the preparatory posture.

(1) At the word of command Semete advances his left foot a pace and assumes the left zenkutsutachi posture, his right fist at his right hip. Then uttering the kiai shout he strikes with his left fist at Ukete's upper body.

Ukete steps back a pace and assumes the right fudotachi posture, his left fist at his left hip, and with the wrist of his right fist springs up his opponent's left hand to ward off the blow (Fig. 159).

Fig. 159

(2) At the word of command Semete assumes the same posture.

Ukete with his right fist at his right hip utters the kiai shout and with his left fist strikes at Semete's middle body (Fig. 160).

(3) At the word of command Semete withdraws his left foot to the preparatory posture.

Ukete steps forward with his left foot and resumes the

preparatory posture. At the close of the foregoing movements Semete and Ukete exchange roles as before and alternating repeat the practice.

URA-NO-6: JODAN-UCHIKOMI-CHUDANTSUKI *(Reverse 6: Upper Step-Strike in—Middle Step-Thrust)*

At the preparatory word of command Semete from the preparatory posture (outer hachijitachi) draws back his right foot a pace and assumes the left zenkutsutachi posture, his right fist at his right hip and his left fist poised for a sweeping lower body blow (gedanbaraitsuki).

Fig. 160

Ukete is in the preparatory posture.

(1)   At the word of command Semete advances a pace with his right foot and assumes the right zenkutsutachi posture, his left fist at his left hip. Then uttering the kiai shout and with his right fist he strikes at Ukete's upper body.

Ukete steps back with his right foot and assumes the left fudotachi posture, his right fist at his right hip. Then brandishing his left fist aloft and using it in the kentsui or hammer fist fashion, or else his wrist, he strikes down his opponent's wrist from above obliquely (Fig. 161).

(2)   At the word of command Semete resumes his posture.

Ukete with his left fist at his left hip utters the kiai shout and with his right fist strikes at his opponent's middle body (chudan) (Fig. 162).

(3)    At the word of command Semete retracts his right foot and assumes the preparatory posture.

Ukete advances his right foot and resumes the preparatory posture.

At the preparatory word of command Semete withdraws

Fig. 161

his left foot a pace and assumes the right zenkutsutachi posture, his left fist at his left hip, and at the same time poises his right fist for a sweeping lower body blow (gedanbaraitsuki).

Ukete is in the preparatory posture.

(1)    At the word of command Semete steps forward and

Fig. 162

assumes the left zenkutsutachi posture. At the same time, his right fist at his right hip, he utters the kiai shout and with his left fist strikes at Ukete's upper body.

Ukete takes a pace backwards and assumes the right

123

fudotachi posture. Then brandishing his right fist as a kentsui or hammer fist, or else with his wrist, he strikes his opponent's wrist downwards in an oblique direction (Fig. 163).

(2) At the word of command Semete resumes his posture.

Ukete with his right fist at his right hip utters the kiai shout and with his left fist strikes at Semete's middle body (Fig. 164).

(3) At the word of command Semete draws back his left foot to the preparatory posture.

Ukete advances his left foot to the preparatory posture.

Afterwards Semete and Ukete exchange roles and repeat the practice. At the end of the demonstration Semete and

Fig. 163

Ukete face each other at a distance between them of about three feet and after having gravely saluted in the prescribed manner turn to the shrine and the Master in charge of the demonstration and repeat the salutation.

The foregoing six forms of kata of the Ten-no-Kata illustrate the so-called Yakusoku Kumite or "agreement kumite" already mentioned. And our Japanese author contends that zealous practice of them will enable you to understand the meaning and purpose of kumite. The kumite kata are of course designed to train you so to move your body as to be ready to cope with a genuine emergency in which your life might be gravely threatened. In this context the following four precepts should therefore be borne in mind: (1) Since the Kumite Kata are intended to apply to real conditions you should study them in that spirit. (2) If you treat them in a frivolous mood you will run the risk of injury and you should therefore practise them in earnest. (3) When you attack your opponent see that you do so for all you are worth with the utmost vim and vigor or, as we say in the vernacular, you must not pull your punches. And if your opponent beats off your attack you should not feel discouraged but remain unperturbed, again concentrate your strength and when it is your turn to act on the defensive then however powerful the attack you should encounter it fully confident in your ability to ward it off. (4) The Ten-no-Kata just described are in

Fig. 164

the first place practised as in every case: two movements of defence and attack respectively, but as you become more proficient you should practise them as a single movement and at the instant of the defence you should already be striking back at your opponent. Perhaps the hard-boiled western student of kinetics may feel disposed to raise his eyebrows on reading this injunction. Doubtless some allowance must be made for over-emphasis, but the sense of the passage probably is that Ukete's "riposte" ensues so swiftly after the defence as to convey the ocular impression of a single action; the two movements merge and coalesce after the bewildering fashion of the crasis in Japanese grammar.

In addition to the Yakusoku Kumite Kata, or "agreement" kumite forms already described, karate recognizes three other classes of kumite called respectively Tanshiki Kumite, or Simple Kumite, Fukushiki Kumite, or Double Kumite, and

125

Jiyu Kumite, or Free Kumite, also called Shiai Kumite, or Contest Kumite. The following brief examples of how these three kumite are executed must suffice:

TANSHIKI KUMITE KATA *(Simple Kumite Kata):* (1) With his right fist A aims a blow at B's face. B recedes a pace with his right foot and as he does so with his left fist, moving powerfully from down upwards, blocks A's right forearm and simultaneously with his right fist aims a blow at A's thorax. Since in this case the method of defence is executed from the inner side of A's body it is technically known as the inner defence, or uchi-uke. (2) Similarly with his right fist A aims a blow at B's face. B recedes a pace with his left foot and holds his right fist in what is technically known as the upper step defence style, or jodan-uke, to all intents and purposes the upper body, and simultaneously with his left fist attacks A's right armpit. Since this defence method is executed from the direction of A's outer body it is known as the outer defence, or soto-uke. A in his turn attacks with his left fist when B retracts his right leg and with his left fist effects an outer defence. The relationship between hand and leg corresponds respectively to that between the middle step defence (chudan-uke) and the lower step defence (gedan-uke). It is imperative that all these movements should be practised by both parties, with exchange of roles, until mastery of them has been achieved.

FUKUKUSHIKI KUMITE KATA *(Double Kumite Kata):* A attacks B and B defends himself and retorts with a counterattack. A in his turn wards off this attack and again attacks B and in this way attack, defence and counter-attack are several times repeated until proficiency is attained. This style of kumite is also graduated into what are called "henka" or variations. These variations range from the second step variation (nidan-henka) to the fourth step variation (yodan-henka) and each successive variation increases in difficulty. The object of this system is to habituate the pupil to every method of defence, attack and counter-attack to a stage at which his action and reaction become almost reflex.

JIYU KUMITE *(Free Kumite):* In contradistinction to the Yakusoku Kumite the partners in the Jiyu Kumite freely apply both offensive and defensive techniques as though engaged in actual combat. But although this form of kumite is optionally styled Jiyu Kumite, Shiai Kumite (Combat

Kumite) and Shinken Kumite (literally "real sword" kumite, otherwise genuine combat kumite), the utmost care must be exercised on both sides to halt the blow or kick a few inches short of the mark, otherwise there would be grave risk of injury to the party at the receiving end! For that reason it is not advisable for novices to engage in Jiyu Kumite but instead to confine themselves to Yakusoku Kumite Kata until their teachers are satisfied that they have acquired a degree of skill sufficient to justify their initiation into Jiyu Kumite.

# CHAPTER IX

## CONCERNING THE VITAL SPOTS IN THE HUMAN BODY AND METHODS OF ATTACKING THEM

IT is essential that every student of karate should familiarize himself with the vital spots (kyusho in Japanese) of the human body. Lacking this knowledge and if engaged in a life and death struggle with a powerful opponent his inability to strike the proper target, i.e. the vital spot, in his opponent's body might lead to his discomfiture and even to a sticky end! In both karate and judo a vital spot may be briefly described as that part of the human body which the karateka assails with hands, fists, wrists, elbows, knees, heels and toes in various ways for the purpose either of knocking out his victim for the count or, if necessary, killing him outright. To this laudable end the utmost precision in locating the vital spot and knowledge of the varying degrees of sensitivity involved in every case are clearly indispensable. This point is emphasized by our Japanese author. Thus if the strength of the attack is inadequate or again if the body of the person attacked has been well tempered, then even if the karateka does hit a vital spot the victim may simply fall but will not be knocked out. Or again, if the attack is weak he may not fall at all. On the other hand, it may easily happen that if a part of the victim's chest, stomach, etc., not even indicated on the kyusho chart, is attacked with a seasoned hand or foot internal haemorrhage can be caused and the victim may die. The ideal to be pursued by the student of karate would seem to be to train to such purpose as never to fail to strike the vital spot and to make his own body so tough that should he by chance fail in his own defence he can withstand the attack without serious injury.

The appended list of names of the vital spots identified in karate, together with the respective methods of attacking them, should be studied in connection with the two charts (Figs. 165a and 165b) on which their positions in the human body, back and front, are clearly indicated. It will be seen

128

from examination of these two charts that in karate as many as forty-four vital spots are identified or considerably more than in the atemiwaza branch of judo. In the appended list all are cited in series against their Japanese names and their nearest

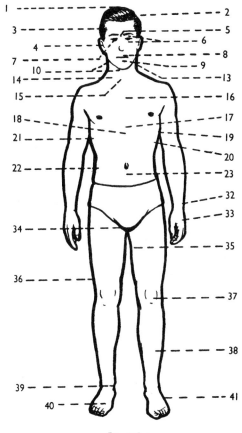

Fig. 165 A

English equivalents. As will be seen from the context not by any means all of these spots are equally vulnerable nor would a karate attack in every instance necessarily prove lethal even though it might seriously disable the victim and deprive him of all further interest in the subsequent proceedings. Yet the residue susceptible to a karate assault meant to kill the victim is sufficiently ample to demonstrate the dangerous potentialities inherent in this formidable art. The karate student will

129

therefore appreciate the importance of caution in his approach to this section and the responsibility devolving upon him never to have recourse to any of these methods unless his own life is threatened by an armed opponent or by superior numbers, armed or unarmed. Here then is the list.

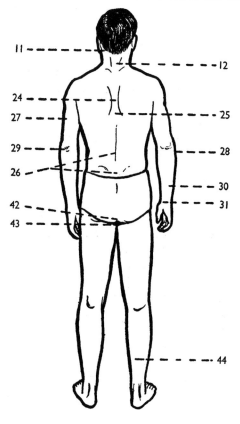

Fig. 165 B

## JODAN KYUSHO
### (Vital Spots in the Upper Part of the Body and Methods of Attack)

1. TENDO (crown of the head): This area extending to the nape of the neck is vulnerable to attack culminating in death. The karate weapons for this purpose include the fist, the kentsui or hammer fist, the tegatana or handsword, more particularly.

130

2. TENTO (the fontanelle or space between the crown of the head and forehead): Highly vulnerable to lethal attack with the fist, the uraken (back fist), tegatana, &c.

3. KOMEKAMI (the temple): Also a very susceptible vital spot which can be effectively attacked with the ipponken, or middle finger fist, the uraken, or back fist, the tegatana, or handsword, &c.

4. MIMI (the ears): Methods of attack identical with No. 3.

5. MIKEN (summit of nose in center of forehead): Area midway between the eyes can be fatally attacked with the fist, the uraken, or back fist, &c.

6. SEIDON (area above and below the eyes): Vulnerable to lethal attack with the nukite, or piercing hand, ipponken, hiraken, or flat or level fist, &c.

7. GANSEI (eyeballs): Can be attacked with the nukite, ipponken, uraken, hiraken, &c.

8. JINCHU (philtrum or spot just under the nose): A highly vulnerable spot familiar to all judo yudansha conversant with atemiwaza. Death can be caused by blows with the fist, uraken, ipponken, tegatana, &c.

9. GEKON (spot beneath the lower lip): Highly vulnerable. If the karateka's punches are not pulled he can kill his opponent with the fist, ipponken, tegatana, &c.

10. MIKAZUKI (the jaw): Attacked with the fist, foot, empi (hiji-ate or elbow blows) described elsewhere.

11. DOKKO (mastoid process behind the ears): Attacked with the fist, ipponken, kentsui, tegatana, &c.

12. KEICHU (nape of neck): Highly vulnerable to blows with the fist, kentsui, ipponken, &c. which may cause death.

### CHUDAN KYUSHO *(Middle Body Vital Spots)*

13. SHOFU (side of neck): Highly vulnerable. Blows with the fist, kentsui, tegatana, empi, &c. may cause death.

14. SONU (spot between throat and top of breastbone or sternum): Very vulnerable. Methods of attack the same as for the Shofu.

15. HICHU (base of throat, Adam's apple or projection of the thyroid cartilage of the larynx): Vulnerable to lethal blows with the fist, empi, knee-cap, kicks, &c.

16. DANCHU (summit of breastbone or sternum): Methods of attack the same as for Hichu.

17. KYOTOTSU (base of breastbone or sternum): Methods of attack the same as for the Hichu.

18. SUIGETSU (solar-plexus): Familiar to all boxers as a highly vulnerable spot. But when subjected to a karate attack with the fist, nukite, empi, knee-cap or kicks, the victim's death can easily ensue.

19. KYOEI (below the armpits, approximately the spot between the fifth and sixth ribs): Another vulnerable area. Death to the victim can ensue from an all-out attack with the fist, empi, kicks, &c.

20. GANCHU (spot below the nipples): Lethally vulnerable. Methods of attack the same as for the Kyoei.

21. DENKO (spot between the seventh and eighth ribs): Lethally vulnerable to attack with the fist, kentsui, tegatana, kicks, &c.

22. INAZUMA (side of body slightly above the hips): Methods of attack the same as for the Denko.

23. MYOJO (spot about an inch below the navel): Another fatal area when attacked with the fist or feet.

24. SODA (spot between the shoulder blades): Very vulnerable when attacked with the fist, empi, &c.

25. KATSUSATSU (spot between the fifth and sixth vertebra): Can be attacked with lethal effect with the same methods as for the Soda.

26. KODENKO (base of spine): Highly vulnerable to blows with the fist and kicks.

27. WANSHUN (back of arm. Top of outside edge of upper arm): Can be attacked with the kentsui, tegatana, &c.

28. HIJIZUME (elbow-joint): Methods of attack the same as for the Wanshun.

29. UDEKANSETSU (arm joint): When effectively applied by a seasoned karateka the kentsui, tegatana, &c. can easily break the joint.

30. KOTE (wrist or back of lower forearm): Effectively applied kentsui, tegatana, empi, &c. can easily fracture the radius of the ulna bones. The ulna is the inner of the two bones of forearm and the radius is the thicker and shorter outer bone.

31. UCHIJAKUZAWA OR MIYAKUDOKORO (inner parts of the

132

forearm where pulsation can be felt): Can be effectively attacked with the fist, ipponken, tegatana, &c.

32. SOTOJAKUZAWA (outer or opposite side to the foregoing): Methods of attack identical.

33. SHUKO (back of the hand): Methods of attack the same as for the Uchijakuzawa.

### GEDAN KYUSHO (Lower Body Vital Spots)

34. KINTEKI (testicles): Can be attacked with fatal effect with the karateka's fist, clutch, knee-cap, kick, &c. The Japanese karate equivalent for our cruder expression euphemistically means "bull's-eye"!

35. YAKO (inside of upper thigh): Can be attacked with the fist or kicked.

36. FUKUTO (outside of lower part of thigh): Methods of attack the same as for the Yako.

37. HIZAKANSETSU (knee-joint): Can be kicked or subjected to fracture by being trodden upon, &c.

38. KOKOTSU (the centre point of the tibia (shin-bone) and fibula (splint bone on outer side of leg)): Can be attacked with the fist, tegatana, &c.

39. UCHIKUROBUSHI (inside of ankle joint): Vulnerable to the kentsui, tegatana, &c.

40. KORI (upper surface of instep): Can be trodden upon with crushing force by a seasoned karateka even with his toughened bare feet.

41. KUSAGAKURE (outside edge of top foot): Methods of attack the same as for the Kori.

42. BITEI (the coccyx, i.e. small triangular bone ending human spinal column): Can be attacked with the knee-cap, kicked, &c. (Fig. 165b).

43. USHIRO-INAZUMA (spot below the buttocks, as shown in Fig. 165b): Can be attacked with the fist, kicked, &c.

44. SOBI (spot on inside of lower part of leg, approximately base of calf): Can be attacked with the fist, kicked, &c.

An important point to be borne in mind in connection with all karate attacks is that after delivery of the attack the natural human weapon used for that purpose, e.g. the foot, knee, elbow, fist, &c., must be instantly withdrawn from the target.

133

# GLOSSARY OF TECHNICAL TERMS

AGETSUKI : Rising Thrust or Blow : Upper-cut.
ASHIGATANA : Footsword.
ASHIKUBI : Ankle.
ASHI-No-Ko : Instep.
ASHI-No-TACHI-KATA : Ways of planting feet.
ASHIURA : Sole of foot.
ASHIWAZA : Leg and foot techniques.
ASHIZOKO : Bottom of foot.
ATEMIWAZA OR ATEWAZA : Methods of attacking vital spots in the human body.
CHOKUSEN-KATA : Straight line kata.
CHOKUTSUKI : Direct Thrust or Blow.
CHUDAN-TEGATANA-UKE : Middle Step (Body) Handsword Defence.
CHUDANTSUKI : Middle Step or Body Thrust or Blow.
CHUDAN-UKE : Middle Step or Body Defence.
DAKITE : Hugging Hand.
EMPI : Elbow attacks.
ENGISEN : Demonstration line.
FUDOTACHI : Immobile Posture.
FUKUSHIKI KUMITE : Double Kumite or Contest Kata.
FUMIKIRI : Step out.
FUMITSUKI : Tread on.
FUMIUCHI : Step Blow.
FURITSUKI : Swinging Thrust or Blow.
GEDANTSUKI : Lower Step or Body Thrust or Blow.
GEDAN-UKE : Lower Step or Body Defence.
GOREI : Word of Command.
GYAKU : Reverse (applied to manner of holding, etc.)
HACHIJITACHI : Figure - Eight Posture.
HARAITE : Sweeping Hand.
HASEN-KATA : Wave-line Kata.
HEISOKUTACHI : Blocked Foot Posture.
HIHO : Secret process, method, formula, &c.
HIJI : Elbow.
HIJIATE : Elbow attacks.
HIKITE : Pull Hand.
HINERITE : Twisting Hand.
HINERI-YOKO-EMPI : Twisting Lateral Empi.
HIRA-HASAMI : Flat Scissors.
HIRAKEN : Flat or Level Fist.
HITOSASHI-YUBI-IPPONKEN : Forefinger Fist.
HIZA : Knee.
HIZAGASHIRA : Knee-cap.
HIZATSUI : Knee Hammer.

134

**J**IYU **K**UMITE : Free Kumite or Contest Kata.

**J**ODANTSUKI : Upper Step or Body Thrust or Blow.

**J**ODAN-**U**KE : Upper Step or Body Defence.

**J**UJI-**U**KE : Figure - Ten Defence.

**K**AKATO : Heel.

**K**AKETE : "Hook Hand".

**K**AKETEBIKI : Special apparatus for training the karateka in various techniques.

**K**AKIWAKE : Thrust aside.

**K**ARATEKA : One who practises karate.

**K**ATA : Pre-arranged Forms of demonstrating methods of attack, defence and counter-attack.

**K**ENTSUI : Hammer Fist.

**K**ERIAGE : Upward Kick.

**K**ERIGAESHI : Return Kick.

**K**ERIHANASHI : Kick release.

**K**ERIKOMI : Kick in.

**K**ERIWAZA : Kicking techniques.

**K**IBATACHI : Equestrian Posture.

**K**OBUSHI : Fist.

**K**O-**E**MPI : Rear Empi.

**K**OKUTSUTACHI : Retroflex Posture.

**K**OSA-**U**KE : Intersecting Defence.

**K**OTE : Forearm.

**K**UMITE : Contest.

**K**YUSHO : Vital spots in the human body. For their names, location and methods of attack see section IX.

**M**AKIWARA : Wooden post to which bundles of straw are bound for training and hardening hands and feet.

**M**AWASHI-**G**ERI : Turning Kick.

**M**IKKATSUKI-**K**ERI : "Three-day moon Kick".

**M**OROTE **C**HUDAN-**U**KE : Both Hands Middle-Step (Body) Defence.

**M**USUBITACHI : Linked Feet Posture.

**N**AGEASHI : Throw Leg.

**N**AIFU-**A**NCHI-**T**ACHI : Anti-Knife Posture.

**N**AKAYUBI-**I**PPONKEN : Middle Finger Fist.

**N**AMIGAESHI : Wave Change.

**N**UKITE : Piercing Hand.

**O**ITSUKI : Pursuit Thrust or Blow.

**R**ENKETSU **R**ENSHUHO : Coupling linking Method of training.

**R**ENZOKUTSUKI : Continuous Blow or Thrust.

**S**AGETA **E**MPI : Lowered Empi.

**S**AGI-**A**SHITACHI : Heron Leg Posture.

**S**ANKAKUTOBI : Triangular Jump.

SAN-NEN-GOROSHI : "Three-year-kill". Alleged secret method of causing deferred death.

SANSENTACHI : Three Battle Posture.

SASAE-UKE : Propping Defence.

SEIKEN : Normal Fist.

SEMETE : Assailant in Kata.

SHICHIDAN-KERI-NO-RENSHUHO : Seven-step Kick Training.

SHIHAN : Teacher, Master, &c.

SHIKOTACHI : Four-thigh Posture.

SHINKO-KATA : Advance or Progress Kata.

SHUTO : Alternative name for Tegatana.

SOTO-UKE : Outer Defence.

SUKUITE : Scooping Hand.

TANSHIKI KUMITE : Simple Kumite or Contest.

TATE-EMPI : Vertical Empi.

TE : Hand.

TEGATANA : Handsword.

TEKUBI : Wrist.

TEWAZA : Hand Techniques.

TOBIGERI : Jumping Kick.

TOBIGOSHI : Jumping over.

TOBIKOMIASHI : Jumping-in Leg.

TO-JIN-HO : Falling person method of training.

TSUKI : Thrust or Blow.

TSUKITE : Thrusting Hand.

UCHITE : Striking Hand.

UCHI-UKE : Inner Defence.

UDE : Arm.

UKE : Defence.

UKETE : Defence Hand.

UKETE : "Receiver" in Karate Kata.

URAKEN : Back Fist.

USHIROGERI : Rear Kick.

WATSUKI : Circle Thrust or Blow.

YAKUSOKU KUMITE : "Agreement" Contest Kata.

YOKO-EMPI : Lateral Empi.

YOKOGERI : Lateral Kick.

YORIASHI : Approaching Leg.

YUBI-HASAMI : Finger Scissors.

YUMI-KOBUSHI : Bow Fist.

YUMI-UKE : Bow Uke or Defence.

ZEN EMPI : Frontal Empi.

ZENGO EMPI : Front and Rear Empi.

ZENKUTSUTACHI : Inclined Posture.

# INDEX

137

*N.B.*—The names of the forty-four vital spots in the human body
have not been indexed separately and can be more conveniently identified in the final section (IX) of the present
Manual.